Joe Biden

Joe Biden

by Michael V. Uschan

LUCENT BOOKS

A part of Gale, Cengage Learning

GALE
CENGAGE Learning™

Detroit • New York • San Francisco • New Haven, Conn • Waterville, Maine • London

LIBRARY OF CONGRESS CATALOGING-IN-PUBLICATION DATA

Uschan, Michael V., 1948-
    Joe Biden / by Michael V. Uschan.
        p. cm. -- (People in the news)
    Includes bibliographical references and index.
    ISBN 978-1-4205-0260-2 (hardcover)
    1. Biden, Joseph R.--Juvenile literature. 2. Vice presidents--United
States--Biography--Juvenile literature. 3. Legislators--United
States--Biography--Juvenile literature. 4. United States.
Senate--Biography--Juvenile literature. I. Title.
    E840.8.B54U83 2010
    352.23'9092--dc22
    [B]
                                                                    2009040739

Lucent Books
27500 Drake Rd
Farmington Hills MI 48331

ISBN-13: 978-1-4205-0260-2
ISBN-10: 1-4205-0260-3

36242060386493

Printed in the United States of America
2 3 4 5 6 7 14 13 12 11 10

Printed by Bang Printing, Brainerd, MN, 2nd Ptg., 07/2010

Contents

Fame and celebrity are alluring. People are drawn to those who walk in fame's spotlight, whether they are known for great accomplishments or for notorious deeds. The lives of the famous pique public interest and attract attention, perhaps because their experiences seem in some ways so different from, yet in other ways so similar to, our own.

Newspapers, magazines, and television regularly capitalize on this fascination with celebrity by running profiles of famous people. For example, television programs such as *Entertainment Tonight* devote all their programming to stories about entertainment and entertainers. Magazines such as *People* fill their pages with stories of the private lives of famous people. Even newspapers, newsmagazines, and television news frequently delve into the lives of well-known personalities. Despite the number of articles and programs, few provide more than a superficial glimpse at their subjects.

Lucent's People in the News series offers young readers a deeper look into the lives of today's newsmakers, the influences that shaped them, and the impact they have had in their fields of endeavor and on other people's lives. The subjects of the series hail from many disciplines and walks of life. They include authors, musicians, athletes, political leaders, entertainers, entrepreneurs, and others who have made a mark on modern life and who, in many cases, will continue to do so for years to come.

These biographies are more than factual chronicles. Each book emphasizes the contributions, accomplishments, or deeds that have brought fame or notoriety to the individual and shows how that person has influenced modern life. Authors portray their subjects in a realistic, unsentimental light. For example, Bill Gates—the cofounder and chief executive officer of the software giant Microsoft—has been instrumental in making the personal computer the most vital tool of the modern age. Few dispute his business savvy, perseverance, or technical expertise, yet critics say he is ruthless in his dealings with competitors and driven more by his desire to maintain Microsoft's dominance in the computer industry than by an interest in furthering technology.

In these books, young readers will encounter inspiring stories about real people who achieved success despite enormous obstacles. Oprah Winfrey—the most powerful, most watched, and wealthiest woman on television today—spent the first six years of her life in the care of her grandparents while her unwed mother sought work and a better life elsewhere. Her adolescence was colored by pregnancy at age fourteen, rape, and sexual abuse.

In every People in the News book, the author documents and supports his or her work with an array of primary and secondary source quotations taken from diaries, letters, speeches, and interviews. All quotes are footnoted to show readers exactly how and where biographers derive their information and provide guidance for further research. The quotations enliven the text by giving readers eyewitness views of the life and accomplishments of each person discussed.

In addition, each book in the series includes photographs, an annotated bibliography, a time line, and a comprehensive index. For both the casual reader and the student researcher, the People in the News series offers insight into the lives of today's newsmakers—people who shape the way we live, work, and play in the modern age.

A Vice President Named Joe

Public officials sometimes become arrogant because of the power they wield in government. They act superior to other people. Vice President Joseph R. Biden has never been arrogant. During the 2008 presidential election, many stories about Biden ran under headlines like "Regular Joe" because the U.S. senator from Delaware has always treated everyone he meets with a casual courtesy that belies his high-ranking position. Even after Biden was elected vice president of the United States on November 4, 2008, he did not want people to call him by his title when they talked to him. Writer John H. Richardson interviewed Biden for a magazine story after Biden was elected but before he took office in January 2009. When Richardson met Biden, he was surprised that Biden wanted to be called by his first name. In his article Richardson recalls their meeting,

> "You can drop the vice-president-elect stuff" [Biden says after Richardson uses that title to greet him].
>
> "Well, I'm not going to call you Joe."
>
> "No, that's all right, you can call me Joe."[1]

The exchange between Biden and Richardson revealed two key facets of the vice president's personality. He does not consider himself better than other people despite the high office he holds, and he loves to talk. The first character trait helped make

Biden popular enough to win seven Senate elections. The second trait, however, has been both a blessing and curse. Biden's ability to talk easily with people he meets, even total strangers, and the ease at which he can speak in front of thousands of people are assets for a political figure. But Biden loves to talk so much that his speeches are sometimes long and rambling, which can bore people, and he has made careless, even stupid remarks that caused him political problems.

However, the most amazing thing about Biden's reputation as someone who loves to talk is that he stuttered so badly when he was a youngster that other children ridiculed him.

A Survivor

The biggest challenge Biden faced while growing up in Scranton, Pennsylvania, and Wilmington, Delaware, was that he stuttered. He even had trouble pronouncing his last name, which could come out as "Bu-Bu-Bu-Biden" when he tried to say it. Because fellow students ridiculed his speech, Biden was determined to stop stuttering. He worked hard to learn to pronounce words properly, and eventually he eliminated his speech impediment. His sister, Valerie Owens, believes Biden's battle with stuttering helped him develop strength of character, an attribute that helped him overcome other obstacles in his life. She recalls,

> I remember him coming home after some of the kids had made fun of the stuttering. But instead of going to a corner and crying, he went into his room, shouting: "I'm going to speak and I'm going to speak directly because that little creep will not make fun of me again." That's the great fire in him we see today.[2]

Biden needed that strength in December 1972 when his wife, Neilia, and infant daughter, Naomi, were killed, and his sons, Hunter and Beau, were severely injured in an auto accident. The tragedy occurred only six weeks after Biden had been elected to his first term as a U.S. senator. Biden was so stricken with grief

Senator Joe Biden earned the nickname "Amtrak Joe" because he used the train to travel from his home in Wilmington to work in Washington, DC.

that he almost resigned his Senate seat. Instead, he persevered and in January 1973 began a distinguished Senate career that lasted more than three decades.

His wife's death led Biden to make an unusual decision. Instead of living in Washington, D.C., like most members of congress, Biden kept his home in Wilmington and commuted to work by train. He did that so family members could help him care for his sons. In his thirty-six years in the Senate, Biden made over seven thousand round-trips by train to perform his Senate duties. The trips, eighty minutes each way, earned Biden the nickname "Amtrak Joe" and solidified his reputation as a public official who did not mind rubbing shoulders with average people.

Biden also survived several other misfortunes in his life. Biden never had trouble being reelected to his Senate seat, but he failed in 1988 and 2008 to win the office he really wanted—president of the United States. His first bid for the presidency ended even before the first primary election when he forgot to credit a British political leader for parts of a campaign speech he gave in Iowa. The accusation that Biden had stolen his speech's content from someone else destroyed his credibility and forced him to quit the race. In early 1988 Biden suffered an even worse setback when a brain aneurysm and other health problems nearly killed him. But Biden fought back through several operations and eight months of rehabilitation to resume his Senate career.

In 2008 Biden failed again to win the Democratic nomination for president. Although some careless remarks he made hurt his campaign early, the main reason he lost was that Senators Hillary Clinton and Barack Obama were much more popular than he was. Biden's dream of attaining higher office seemed shattered when he withdrew from the race after the first primary in January 2008. Then Obama won the nomination, and he chose Biden as his vice presidential running mate.

Obama picked Biden because he respected his experience, especially in foreign affairs. However, Obama worried that Biden might say something that could hurt the campaign because of verbal goofs he had made in the past. Biden did not make any major slips, but a careless comment in a television interview on

September 22, 2008, did make him look a bit silly. In discussing the weakening U.S. economy, Biden tried to explain how President Franklin D. Roosevelt calmed the economic fears people had during the Great Depression in the 1930s. Biden said, "When the stock market crashed, Franklin D. Roosevelt got on the television and didn't just talk about the, you know, the princes of greed [investment brokers]. He said, 'Look, here's what happened.' "[3] Biden should have said "radio" instead of "television" because televisions did not exist yet. But Biden once again survived a verbal gaffe, and he and Obama were elected on November 4, 2008.

Never Give Up

Biden survived all the ups and downs of his life and political career to become the nation's forty-seventh vice president. In his 2007 memoir, *Promises to Keep: On Life and Politics*, Biden explains

Biden, with President Barack Obama, overcame many challenges before becoming vice president. He credits the lesson of "never give up" for his success.

that everything he has accomplished is due to a lesson he learned early in life. The lesson was to never give up no matter what happened. Biden writes,

> The art of living is simply getting up after you've been knocked down. After the surgery [for an aneurysm], Senator, you might lose the ability to speak? Get up! [Your] wife and daughter, I'm sorry, Joe, there was nothing we could do to save them? Get up! Kids make fun of you because you stutter, Bu-bu-bu-bu-bu-Biden? Get up![4]

Chapter 1

Raised in a Loving Family

Joe Biden attended the seventh grade at Saint Helena's, a Roman Catholic elementary school in Wilmington, Delaware. Biden stuttered when he was young, and one day when he stumbled over words while reading out loud in class, the teacher, who was also a nun, mocked him by calling him "Mr. Bu-bu-bu-bu-Biden." The seventh grader was so angry and embarrassed that he fled the classroom and walked 2 miles (3.2km) home. The school called his mother, Jean, to explain what happened. As soon as Joe arrived home, she drove him back to school to meet with the principal and his teacher. When the nun admitted she had called him "Mr. Bu-bu-bu-bu-Biden," Jean walked up to the nun and said, "If you ever speak to my son like that again, I'll come back and rip that bonnet off your head. Do you understand me?"[5] A bonnet is the religious habit that nuns wore on their head back then. It includes a cowl that covered their hair and the sides of their faces. Mrs. Biden then ordered Joe to go back to class, and she went home.

The passionate reaction to a teacher who hurt her son is an example of the strong role Biden's mother played in his life. Both of Biden's parents were loving and fiercely protective of their son. They taught him to be loyal to friends and family, to never give up, and to treat everyone with respect. Such lessons and those from other family members helped shape the man who would become vice president of the United States.

Lessons Learned

Joseph Robinette Biden Jr. was born on November 20, 1942, in Scranton, Pennsylvania. His parents, Joseph Robinette Biden Sr. and Catherine Eugenia "Jean" Finnegan, had three more children after Joseph Jr. was born—two sons, James Brian and Francis "Frank" W., and a daughter, Valerie.

Biden Sr. worked as an executive for a company that sold sealants to ships. The Biden family was well-to-do and lived in a nice home in a Boston, Massachusetts, suburb. Biden Sr. had grown up in a rich family, and as a young man, he flew airplanes and sailed yachts. His father had a high-level position with the giant oil company Amoco and was friends with the founders of the company.

Joe Biden grew up in Scranton, Pennsylvania, with his family. Shown here is a part of downtown Scranton.

When World War II ended in 1945, Biden Sr. decided to open a furniture store with a partner. The plan failed when the partner stole money they had pooled to buy a building. Biden and another friend then bought a small airfield on Long Island, New York, and began a crop-dusting business whereby airplanes spray insecticide on apple orchards and potato farms to safeguard crops. When that business failed in 1947, Biden Sr. was so broke that he and his family had to live with his wife's grandparents, Ambrose and Geraldine Finnegan, in Scranton. The Finnegan's had a two-story home in Green Ridge, which was one of Scranton's better neighborhoods and was heavily populated by Irish Americans.

Living with his wife's family was a humbling experience for a man who had always made a lot of money and enjoyed a life of relative luxury. Biden Sr. had trouble finding work but eventually began cleaning boilers for a heating and cooling company and doing other low-paying jobs. Joe Biden Jr. said his father never became depressed or felt sorry for himself because of the business failures that changed his life. Biden Jr. recalls, "My dad always said, 'Champ, the measure of a man is not how often he is knocked down, but how quickly he gets up'"[6] That was one of the most important lessons Joe learned from a father who lovingly called his first-born son "Champ."

The Bidens were so poor that Biden Jr. sometimes had to put a piece of cardboard in the bottom of his shoes to cover holes. Although the Bidens could not give their children many material things, the love and devotion they showered on them made them feel confident in themselves. "My mother and father," Biden Jr. says, "always reinforced the notion that there wasn't anything I couldn't do."[7] They also taught Biden Jr. lessons about how he should act, such as being loyal to friends and family members. Once when Biden Jr. was a safety patrol lieutenant, his sister misbehaved on the bus that took them to school. Knowing he should report his sister to school officials but not wanting to, Biden Jr. asked his dad what he should do. "Well, Joey," Biden Sr. said, "you know that's not your only option."[8] The next day Biden Jr. quit the patrol so he would not have to get his sister into trouble.

Biden Jr. slept in an attic bedroom with sloped ceilings in his grandparents' home, which was always filled with family members and friends. After Mass on Sunday, they would all crowd around the Finnegans' kitchen table and discuss sports and politics. Biden Jr. always listened intently when they discussed local

Joe "Impedimenta"

In his book, *Promises to Keep: On Life and Politics*, Joe Biden recalls how fellow students taunted him because he stuttered. He writes,

> Joe Impedimenta. My classmates hung that nickname on me our first semester of high school. It was one of the first big words we learned [in Latin class]. Impedimenta— the baggage that impedes one's progress. So I was Joe Impedimenta. Or Dash. [They] didn't call me Dash because of what I could do on the football field; they called me Dash because I talked like Morse code. Dot-dot-dot-dot-dash-dash-dash-dash. "You gu-gu-gu-gu-guys sh-sh-sh-sh-shut up!" My impedimenta was a stutter. It wasn't always bad. When I was at home with my brothers and sister, hanging out with my neighborhood friends, or shooting the bull on the ball field, I was fine, but when I got thrown into a new situation or a new school, had to read in front of the class, or wanted to ask out a girl, I just couldn't do it. [Other] kids looked at me like I was stupid. They laughed. I wanted so badly to prove I was like everybody else. Even today I can remember the dread, the shame, the absolute rage, as vividly as the day it was happening. There were times I thought it was the end of the world, my impedimenta. I worried that the stutter was going to be my epitaph. And there were days I wondered: How would I ever beat it?

Joe Biden, *Promises to Keep: On Life and Politics*, New York: Random House, 2007, p. 3.

and national political events. Those talks were still so vivid in his memory six decades later that he describes them in *Promises to Keep: On Life and Politics*, the memoir he wrote in 2007. During a book signing in his old hometown, Biden told a reporter: "I never intended to write about Scranton. I intended to write about my political philosophy and how it was formed, and it turns out it was formed here in my grandfather's kitchen."[9]

Overcoming the Stutter

Joe Biden stuttered when he was young, and it was not a serious problem until he began going to school. Before that, the young boy's friends and family had accepted him and he was not embarrassed by his halting speech pattern. But Biden's stuttering grew worse in school because he was nervous talking in front of people he did not know. When fellow students mocked him, he became embarrassed and angry, and then he would stutter even more. His mother tried to ease his pain saying, "Joey, it's because you're so bright you can't

It is remarkable that Joe Biden, who as a youngster had a problem with stuttering, grew up to be a man who gives speeches in front of thousands.

get the thoughts out quickly enough."[10] The Bidens took their son to a speech pathologist when he was in kindergarten but the therapist failed to help him correct his speech impediment.

In 1953 when Biden was ten years old, his family moved to Delaware because his father was having trouble finding work in Scranton. Biden Sr. found a good job as a car salesman, and after living in a small apartment for a few years, the family was able to buy a home. The Bidens began to enjoy their new life but Biden Jr. still stuttered. When he began attending an all-boys high school, students cruelly called him "Dash," because his stopping and starting while talking sounded more like Morse code than normal speech. They also called him "Joe Impedimenta," because stuttering is a speech impediment. Biden tried to ignore the taunting. His athletic prowess in sports and likable personality helped him make friends and ease some of the kidding about how he spoke, but he sometimes used his fists to quiet his tormentors.

Many of Biden's teachers tried to help him with his stuttering by giving him tips on how to talk correctly, and they defended him in class when students mocked him. None of them, however, was able to help him stop stuttering, and by the time he got to high school, his stuttering had become such a liability that he became determined to do something about it.

One reason Biden felt compelled to overcome his stuttering was that his uncle Edward Finnegan, who was nicknamed "Boo-Boo," also stuttered badly. Finnegan, who lived with the Biden family for many years, told Joe once that he had wanted to be a doctor when he was growing up but did not go to medical school because he stuttered. "I loved Uncle Boo-Boo," Biden writes in his memoir, "but I knew I never wanted to end up like him."[11] Biden licked his stuttering by memorizing long lines of poetry and then reciting them over and over again to repeat sounds he had trouble speaking correctly. He explains,

> The things I wanted to be, I worried I could never be because I couldn't talk. I'd stand in front of the mirror and repeat Emerson's "Meek young men grow up in libraries, believing it their duty," watching the muscles in my face. I knew I had to talk. I knew I had to overcome this.[12]

By sheer willpower and practice, Biden smoothed out his speech pattern and was able to quit stuttering. But even as an adult, Biden admits "I have never forgotten what it was like and how tough it is for anyone who's had to face it."[13]

Family Lessons

Joe Biden's parents taught him many lessons about life. One lesson came at his dad's company Christmas party, when his dad was working for an auto dealership. During the party, the dealership's owner had a bucket full of silver dollars and he tossed the coins on the floor. Then he watched in amusement as his employees scrambled for the coins. Joe Biden Sr. believed the act humiliated the workers, so he left the party with his family and quit his job. In 2008 when Biden accepted the Democratic nomination for vice president, he spoke about his parents and what they taught him. In his speech he said,

> You know, my mom taught her children—all the children who flocked to our house [when he was growing up]—that you're defined by your sense of honor and you're redeemed by your loyalty. She believes that bravery lives in every heart, and her expectation is that it will be summoned. Failure—failure at some point in your life is inevitable, but giving up is unforgivable. My mother's creed is the American creed: No one is better than you. Everyone is your equal, and everyone is equal to you. My parents taught us to live our faith and to treasure our families. We learned the dignity of work, and we were told that anyone can make it if they just try hard enough. That was America's promise. And for those of us who grew up in middle-class neighborhoods like Scranton and Wilmington, that was the American dream.

Joe Biden, speech, Democratic National Convention, Denver, CO, August 27, 2008, www.foxnews.com/politics/elections/2008/08/27/raw-data-transcript-of-joe-bidens-speech-at-democratic-convention.

Senator Chuck Hagel dresses up as Joe Biden for Halloween and shakes the real senator's hand. Biden learned from his family to treat all people as equals. His "regular Joe" personality appeals to many people.

Sports and Lots of Friends

Although speaking normally made Biden feel better about himself and made it easier for him to socialize with other students, he had never lacked friends, even when he was stumbling over his words while talking. As an adult, Biden reminisces about the things he and his friends liked to do in Scranton in the 1940s. He says "Once we spent our limit on penny candy from Simmey's [their favorite candy store], Charlie Roth, Larry Orr, Tommy Bell and I would head down to the Roosie (Roosevelt) Theatre for the 12-cent, double-feature usually a pair of westerns or a Tarzan."[14] Biden did not even have to leave home to have fun with his friends because they always enjoyed coming to his house. They came not just to play with their buddy Joe but to talk to his mother. She was so sympathetic that the boys would discuss problems with her that they would never have the courage to talk about with their own mother. Biden says that when his friends

A New York Yankees pitcher warms up before a game in the 1940s. Although Biden suffered from a stutter as a child, he felt confident playing games like baseball and football.

came over to talk with his Mom "we [he and his siblings] would say, 'Mom is hearing confession again.'"[15]

Biden made lots of friends because he was a good athlete as well as a daredevil who was not afraid to try dangerous stunts just to see if he could do them. Jim Kennedy, a friend who lived along an alley near Biden's home, says, "You couldn't dare him to do anything, because the problem was he'd do it. His DNA is still up in that alley, because I never saw anybody bleed as much as him [after doing some foolish stunt]."[16] Biden once climbed atop a smoldering mountain of coal refuse that was shaky and could have toppled over and burned him, and another time he ran underneath a moving piece of heavy machinery. Biden admits that his embarrassment over stuttering led him to do dangerous things to prove his bravery and make people accept him.

The mental toughness and physical agility that enabled Biden to perform such daredevil stunts also made him a good athlete. He was a star in football and other sports in high school, and he and his friends were always playing pick-up games of baseball and other sports. In his memoir Biden writes,

As much as I lacked confidence in my ability to communicate verbally, I always had confidence in my athletic ability. Sports was as natural to me as speaking was unnatural. And sports turned out to be my ticket to acceptance. I wasn't easily intimidated in a game, so even when I stuttered, I was always the kid who said "Give me the ball."[17]

Enough Alcoholics

Joe Biden does not drink alcohol. The reason is that some members of his family have become alcoholics because they could not control their drinking. In a biographical story on Biden in the *New York Times* newspaper during the 2008 presidential campaign, reporter John M. Broder explains Biden's family history with alcohol. He writes,

Though Joe [Biden] Sr. was not a heavy drinker, alcohol flowed freely in the Finnegan house and in the neighborhood. Joe Jr. saw the toll it took on his family, his neighbors and, later, on his little brother Frankie [Francis W. Biden]. "Every family had it," said Tom Bell, one of Senator Biden's childhood friends from Scranton who remains close to him. "But the Finnegans had more than their share." Senator Biden does not drink at all, and he is frank about the reason. "There are enough alcoholics in my family," he said last month as he sipped cranberry juice on a train ride from Washington to Wilmington.

John M. Broder, "Father's Tough Life an Inspiration for Biden," *New York Times*, October 23, 2008, www.nytimes.com/2008/10/24/us/politics/24biden.html?_r=1.

Archmere Academy

When it came time to choose a high school, Biden only had to look out of his second-story window to see what he called "the object of my deepest desire, my Oz."[18] What Biden was able to view from his bedroom was Archmere Academy, a prestigious Roman Catholic prep school.

Archmere was known for its successful sports programs, and Biden dreamed of playing sports there. Tuition, however, was three hundred dollars a year. Biden could have gone to a public school for free or another private school for less money, but he had his heart set on Archmere. He talked his father into letting him go there by agreeing to work for the school during the summer pulling weeds, washing windows, painting fences, and doing other jobs. The school allowed students to do that in return for a reduction in their tuition.

Biden's freshman year was marred at first by the fact that he was very small for his age. The fourteen-year-old freshman was only 5-feet, 1-inch (1.5m) tall and weighed just 100 pounds (45kg). But Biden grew a foot before graduating in June 1961, and his new size combined with his athletic ability let him play basketball, football, and basketball at Archmere. Biden was especially good in football—he was a running back and wide receiver—and in his senior year he led Archmere to an undefeated season. Decades later E. John Walsh, his football coach, fondly remembered Biden. He said, "He was a skinny kid but he was one of the best pass receivers I had in 16 years as a coach."[19]

The tall but slim player made up for his lack of bulk by being more competitive than his opponents. Teammate Marty Londergan, however, claims Biden was sometimes too competitive. Biden liked taunting opposing players, and Londergan said players and fans sometimes got so angry at him that Archmere players feared they would be attacked before they could leave the football field.

Biden enjoyed the accolades he won in sports, but as an adult, he claims that his proudest high school accomplishment was learning to speak correctly. "Overcoming my stuttering," Biden says, "taught me one of the most important lessons in my life; that if you put your mind to something, there's nothing you can't do."[20]

Chapter 2

College, Marriage, and Politics

In 1961 Joe Biden graduated from Archmere Academy and enrolled in the University of Delaware. Like many young men at the time, Biden was the first in his family to go to college. Many young men and women were encouraged to go to college by their parents, who told their children that a good education was the key to getting better jobs, making more money, and having a better life than they had.

One of those parents was Joe Biden Sr. Even though Biden Sr. had not gone to college himself, he kept telling his son that a college degree would help him realize any dreams he had in life. And Biden Jr. already had one—he wanted to become an elected official. In his memoir Biden writes,

> Like a lot of teenagers, I had outlandish … daydreams that filled my head in high school. [One] was to become an esteemed public figure—who would do great things and earn a place in the history books … on the good side.[21]

Biden's dream of public service began as a young boy in Scranton, Pennsylvania, when he listened to his grandfather and other family members debate politics. His determination to become an elected official was strengthened in 1960 when John F. Kennedy became the first Roman Catholic president. Kennedy became a political hero to Biden and many other young Americans. Biden was especially inspired by Kennedy's inaugural address, in which Kennedy

The First Catholic President

John F. Kennedy was the first Roman Catholic president of the United States. His election on November 8, 1960, was heartening to Catholics like Joe Biden because some Americans disliked Catholics. This sentiment was so strong at this time that some political experts believed it would be hard for a Catholic to be elected president. Kennedy eased fears about his religion in a speech on September 12, 1960, to the Greater Houston (Texas) Ministerial Association, when he

President John F. Kennedy and his wife Jacqueline in 1960.

discussed the nation's greatness and the need to keep the United States strong against its enemies. Biden writes, "What he said was a powerful public confirmation of the things I'd learned growing up: What we valued most—equity, fairness, and simple justice—were ours to protect, not God's."[22] The fact that Kennedy was Catholic also assured Biden that his religion would not hurt him when he sought election even though there had been lingering anti-Catholic sentiment in parts of the nation when he was growing up.

Kennedy had originally become successful in politics because of his father's wealth and political connections. Biden had neither of those advantages, so he began studying how people who came

continued

vowed not to let his religion influence decisions he made as president. Kennedy told Protestant leaders his Roman Catholic faith would not affect his conduct as president. He said,

> I believe in an America where the separation of church and state is absolute—where no Catholic prelate would tell the President (should he be Catholic) how to act, and no Protestant minister would tell his parishioners for whom to vote—where no church or church school is granted any public funds or political preference—and where no man is denied public office merely because his religion differs from the President who might appoint him or the people who might elect him. I believe in an America that is officially neither Catholic, Protestant nor Jewish…. I am not the Catholic candidate for President. I am the Democratic Party's candidate for President who happens also to be a Catholic. I do not speak for my church on public matters—and the church does not speak for me.

John F. Kennedy, speech to the Greater Houston Ministerial Association, September 12, 1960, Houston, TX, www.americanrhetoric.com/speeches/jfkhoustonministers.html.

from average families were able to win elections. When Biden discovered most of them had been lawyers, he decided his first step toward realizing his dream was to become a lawyer.

A Lazy Student

Biden studied history and political science at the University of Delaware. To the disappointment of his father, Biden had not been a good student in high school and had received mostly C grades. "I was looking for Bs, a C-plus," Biden Sr. said of his son. "Joe was never a knock-down, drag-out scholar. That's for

In 1961, Biden began college at the University of Delaware, pictured. He wanted to become a public official.

sure. He was primarily interested in girls and sports."[23] Biden Jr.'s academic pattern continued in college despite his goals of becoming a lawyer and entering politics.

The transition from high school to college was difficult for Biden and his first semester was especially rough. "I did not do very well," Biden admits. "I ended up with a 1.9 [grade point average], [and it] put me on probation."[24] The problem was that Biden spent more time dating and playing for the freshman football team than studying.

Biden's father was so angry about his son's poor grades that he made him quit playing football. Even though Biden began to pay more attention to his studies, he did not work very hard during his first two years in college because he believed all he had to do was pass courses and graduate to get into law school. And because Biden had the ability to study at the last minute for his final examinations and still pass the tests, he was able to pass his courses without studying much during the semester. That ability won him the admiration of his friends but hurt his academic standing, because his grades were not very good.

At the start of his junior year Biden, like many young people nearing graduation, became worried about his future and decided to talk to one of his political science professors about what he needed to do to get into law school. The professor told Biden he had to work harder his final three semesters to make up for his lackadaisical effort thus far. Faced with the reality that he had endangered his life's dream, Biden decided to become a serious student. He says, "Once I made that commitment, I did it. I carried thirty-seven hours the next two semesters with decent grades."[25]

In 1964 after Biden had nearly finished the first of those grueling semesters, he went to Nassau in the Bahamas on spring break. He met someone during that vacation who changed his life.

Falling in Love

Biden originally drove to Fort Lauderdale, Florida, for spring break. But when a friend asked him to go to Paradise Island in Nassau, the Bahamas—the plane ride was only $25—he decided to spend his vacation there. He and Fred Sears stayed at a house

While on vacation in the Bahamas in 1964, Biden met and fell in love with Neilia Hunter, left. They married in 1966.

being rented by some other students they knew. The first day they were in Nassau, he and Sears saw two young women sitting by the pool of the British Colonial Hotel. One of them was blond and the other was brunette. Biden remembers arguing with Sears over which of them he would talk to: "I said to my friend, 'I get the blond.' So we ended up flipping a coin and I won [and] Neilia and I hit it off immediately."[26] Even though only hotel guests were allowed to use the pool, Biden calmly walked through the pool area and started talking to Neilia Hunter, a Syracuse University student who was also on spring break.

After the two students talked for a long time by the pool, Biden asked Hunter to go to dinner. Hunter chose the restaurant but when the bill came, it was twenty dollars, three dollars more than Biden had. When Biden admitted that he did not have enough money to pay the bill and how embarrassed he was, Hunter said, "Don't be. That happens a lot to my dad. You shouldn't be embarrassed."[27] Her sympathetic understanding of the situation was one of the things that made Biden fall in love with Hunter.

Biden spent all of his time the next three days with Hunter. When Biden went home for the final days of his vacation, he told his family and all his friends that he had found the girl he wanted to marry. During summer vacation that year, Biden drove 320 miles (515km) each weekend to visit Hunter at her parents' home in Skaneateles, New York. They began to think about getting married, but there was a problem. The Hunters were Presbyterian and Neilia's father asked her to quit seeing Biden because he was Catholic. But when she told her father she did not want to have to choose between her family and the man she loved, her father relented and allowed the relationship to continue. During the last month of summer vacation, Biden worked at a marina in Skaneateles and he and Hunter were together every day.

That fall Biden returned to school and worked harder than ever so he could be a success and marry Hunter. But Biden still found time to keep visiting Hunter, who had graduated and was teaching in Skaneateles. Biden either borrowed a car to make trip or hitchhiked so he could be with her. Biden graduated in 1965 with a less-than-sterling academic record. He finished 506th in his

Joe and Neilia

It was love at first sight in 1964 when Joe Biden met Neilia Hunter. It was Hunter who made Biden believe he could realize his dream of being an elected official. In his book, *Promises to Keep: On Life and Politics*, Biden writes,

> I'd be a trial lawyer and build my own firm, then run for public office. Once I had Neilia with me, it became more of a plan than a daydream. Nobody outside my family had ever believed in me the way Neilia did; seeing myself through her eyes made anything seem possible. Now I could see the picture whole, the law firm, the campaign announcement, the speeches, the travel, the victory night, and being in office, being of service. Seeing it meant seeing it all the way to the end. And I could see the moves. I knew how Neilia and I would look, what I'd say, what I wanted to do in office. When I told Neilia I didn't just talk about holding office, I talked about using the office to make things better for people. And Neilia agreed. "[We] can do this" was how she'd say it. "I promise you."

Joe Biden, *Promises to Keep: On Life and Politics*, New York: Random House, 2007, p. 33.

graduating class of 688 students, but he was accepted by Syracuse University College of Law. He applied to Syracuse because it was located close to Hunter's hometown.

Law School and Marriage

Law school was key to Biden's dream for his future, but he continued his lazy study habits because he still did not enjoy going to class. "The work didn't seem so hard, just boring," Biden says, "and I was a dangerous combination of arrogant and sloppy."[28]

In the 1960s protests against the Vietnam War were very common on college campuses, but Biden did not let himself become distracted from his law studies.

As Biden had done at the University of Delaware, he skipped a lot of classes. He also wasted valuable study time by starting a team in an intramural football league. Biden's ability to study at the last minute for examinations and help from Hunter helped him get passing grades in most of his classes. However, his poor work habits caused him to flunk one class. That mistake nearly got him expelled from school.

Lawyers have to learn how to write a variety of legal papers and how to cite various legal decisions and laws. In his freshman year, Biden flunked a writing course because he was accused of plagiarizing, or copying, passages from an article by the journal, *Fordham Law Review*. Copying someone else's work and claiming it as your own is so serious an offense that the school considered expelling him. Biden had to meet with law school officials and explain that he had only failed to properly identify the work that he used in his paper, which would have made it all right to use. Biden admits that he had skipped so many classes that he never learned how to properly identify and credit material he included in his schoolwork. "If I had taken law school seriously, and didn't screw around," Biden said years later, "I would have known how to footnote the paper."[29] Biden was allowed to take the course again the next semester and passed.

After his near-disastrous first year at Syracuse, Biden married Hunter on August 27, 1966. The marriage helped Biden focus on his studies in his final two years of law school. During this period, the Vietnam War was at its peak. Many students at Syracuse and other colleges across the nation were involved in protests against the war, some of which were violent. Biden was never involved in

Joe Biden and the Vietnam War

The United States was involved in the Vietnam War from 1959 to April 30, 1975, when its final soldiers were evacuated from South Vietnam. The war divided the United States politically for more than a decade because over fifty-eight thousand U.S. soldiers died in the conflict. The war was also controversial because the federal government drafted several million men and forced them to join the military and fight in the war even if they did not want to. Joe Biden was not drafted because he received five deferments because he was a student. Just before Biden graduated from law school and would no longer be a student, he was required to take a physical on April 5, 1968. He was then declared physically unfit for military service because he had asthma when he was younger. Biden once told a newspaper reporter that if he had been drafted, he would have joined the military but that, like many young men his age, he had not been eager to go to war. He said, "I was prepared to go. I was not anxious to go, because I didn't think, 'My God, I can hardly wait to go and join the military.'"

Quoted in Lois Romano, "Joe Biden and the Politics of Belief; Ready to Announce for President, He Dismisses the Polls: 'I'm Going to Win,'" *Washington Post*, June 9, 1987.

the antiwar demonstrations. He says, "It [protesting] wasn't going on when I was in college, and when I was in [law] school I wasn't hanging around at the student union. I was hanging around with other married couples."[30] Biden claims he had reservations about whether U.S. participation in the war was justified but had never felt strongly enough to join protests against the conflict that was politically dividing the nation.

In 1968 Biden received his law degree from Syracuse University College of Law. Even though Biden finished only seventy-sixth out of eighty-five students in his class, he soon began working as a lawyer in Wilmington, Delaware.

A Lawyer and Elected Official

Biden was hired out of law school to work for a law firm that had rich corporate clients, like railroads and oil companies. However, he soon became disenchanted with the work. Biden quit after the firm represented a company that was sued by one of its workers, a welder who had been injured in a job-related accident. The law firm used legal maneuvers so the company would not have to pay the welder any damages, even though he had been seriously hurt. That seemed unfair to Biden, who had come from a working-class family. The case made him change his mind about what kind of lawyer he wanted to be. He writes, "I felt like I should be representing the plaintiff, that my place was with people who were outside the reach of the system."[31]

Biden then took a job as a public defender, representing people charged with crimes who could not afford an attorney. He also began working part-time for an attorney named Sidney Balick, representing average people in civil lawsuits. Biden later opened his own law office with David Walsh, a college friend. Even though Biden was busy with his law practice, he became directly involved in politics for the first time by joining the Democratic Forum. The forum was a group of young, liberal Democrats trying to change the conservative policies of the Delaware Democratic Party. The forum wanted the party to support school integration and open housing for blacks.

Forum members were so impressed with Biden's ideas and personality that in 1970 they asked him to run for the New Castle County Council. Although the council district in which Biden lived was 60 percent Republican, his fellow Democrats thought Biden was a strong enough candidate to have a chance at winning the election. Biden had always thought he would not enter politics until he was more established in his career and had done more to make himself known in the community. But after talking it over with his wife and other family members, Biden decided to enter the race.

Biden's campaign effort was a family affair. His sister, Valerie, ran his campaign, his mother hosted coffee parties for voters, and his wife helped him plan his campaign tactics. Biden referred to Neilia as the "brains" of his campaign because she came up with so many ideas about what he should do to win votes. Walsh said she was effective in making Biden accept her ideas because "she could control him and make him think it was his idea."[32] What helped Biden win the election more than anything else was his relentless door-to-door campaigning to convince people to vote for him, especially in middle-class areas that usually supported Republican candidates. Even though the district Biden lived in was predominantly Republican, as was most of Delaware, Biden got two-thousand votes more than his opponent to win the county council election on November 3, 1970.

"Faster than Expected"

Biden's county council victory added to the success and happiness he was experiencing just a few years after graduating from college. He was working as an attorney, had a wife he loved, and was already a proud father of three children. Joseph R. "Beau" Biden III was born in 1969, Robert Hunter in 1970, and Naomi Christina in 1971. But his victory was only a modest first step toward the dream of political greatness which he began nurturing as a young boy. When Biden was still a junior in college and getting to know his wife's parents, Neilia's mother asked him what he wanted to be. When Biden answered "President," she did not

Even as a young attorney, Biden knew he wanted to become president of the United States.

seem to know what he meant, so he quickly added "of the United States."[33] It was a huge dream, one his mother-in-law at first failed to comprehend because it seemed so extravagant. But by 1970, Biden had already taken a first small step toward reaching it.

Chapter 3

Triumph and Tragedy

In 1967 while Biden was attending Syracuse University College of Law, he and Neilia bought a puppy and named it Senator. Biden hoped the dog's name would be an omen of the type of high-level political position he would hold one day. Only four years later, Biden had begun his political career as a member of the New Castle County Council. Biden enjoyed his council position even though it entailed a lot of boring work, such as considering plans for construction of roads or sewers. But one issue that did excite Biden was to make sure big companies moving into the area would not hurt the environment when they built new factories.

The council position was only a small step toward Biden's goal of holding an office in which he would wield enough power to change government to be more responsive to the needs of average people. But Biden was happy at how quickly he had begun realizing his dreams for a career and family. Biden writes that after the 1970 council election, "Neilia and I could both feel our life beginning to pick up speed. Everything was happening faster than expected."[34] What Biden could not foresee was how much more rapidly he would advance politically.

A Long-Shot Candidate

Biden's participation in the Delaware Democratic Party led to his involvement in an attempt to recruit a candidate to challenge Republican senator J. Caleb Boggs in the 1972 election. Nobody, however, wanted to run against Boggs because he was so popular. He had not only been a senator since 1961 but he also had previously been governor of Delaware from 1953 to 1960 and a U.S. representative before that.

In the summer of 1971, Biden attended the party's annual convention in Dover, Delaware. Biden was in his motel room when two party officials visited him. To Biden's surprise, Henry Topen and Bert Carvel asked him to run against Boggs. The request stunned Biden, who was not sure if he had the experience or was even old enough to legally be a senator. Under the U.S. Constitution, a member of Congress has to be at least thirty years old, and Biden would not turn thirty until November 20, 1972. But the officials told him he only had to be that age by January 3, 1973, the day he would take office if he won, and so they asked him to run.

Biden says he knew the officials thought Boggs was unbeatable. He writes, "I don't think they thought I could win. They thought I'd present a decent case, I'd be a decent candidate."[35] Even though Biden was not sure himself that he could win, he knew such a high-profile election would help him in the future by making his name known throughout the state. Biden also realized that if he did win, he would have real power to change government policies he did not like.

Before deciding to run, Biden discussed the subject with friends and family members. Ted Kaufman was skeptical about his chances. Kaufman says that when Biden asked for his support, "I said I would, but I said, 'Joe, I've got to be honest with you; I really don't think you have much of a chance to win this race.'"[36] Childhood friend Jim Kennedy also told Biden he thought he would lose because Delaware was strongly Republican. Kennedy says "[Biden] looked at me and said, 'I can talk now.'"[37] The young boy who had mastered his stutter now believed he could speak well enough to convince people to vote for him.

The support Biden needed most was from his own family. When they all said they would help, Biden decided to challenge Boggs.

Valerie Biden Owens

Joe Biden's sister, Valerie Biden Owens, was a feminist pioneer in political campaigning. When Owens managed Biden's 1972 U.S. Senate campaign, she was one of the first women to head such an important campaign. Owens went on to manage all her brother's campaigns, including his 2008 bid to win the Democratic nomination for president. In a newspaper interview in 2009, Owens commented on how rare

Valerie Biden Owens managed Joe Biden's campaign for the Senate in 1972. She continued to campaign on his and Barack Obama's behalf in 2008.

that opportunity was in 1972 and how some men she encountered were condescending to her because she was a woman. She said,

> So I was a rare sighting and at best, I was considered high risk. My start in politics was strictly personal. He [Biden] and I could complete each other's sentences, and 99 percent of the time, we reached the same conclusion. [He] was never intimidated by women, and least of all by his baby sister, but rather he was in awe. He was patient and generous, and he always encouraged me to reach and try harder and work and play fairly. [One campaign consultant] in particular told me, as he put his hand on my thigh, to not worry my pretty little head anymore about these ads. That was his job, and why didn't I get back to organizing the volunteers. But Joe made it clear from the beginning that no ad, no printed material, no brochure was going to go out from the campaign without my approval.

Quoted in Jennifer Price, "VP's Sister, Adviser Managed His Campaigns," *News Journal (DE),* April 5, 2009, www.delawareonline.com/article/20090405/NEWS02/904050354/1006/NEWS.

A Family Affair

Biden announced his candidacy in March 1972. His bid to unseat Boggs was an uphill battle because he had very little money, no experience running a statewide campaign, and was almost unknown by Delaware voters. Biden's biggest strength was his family. He chose his sister, Valerie Owens, to run his campaign because they were so close and because she had done a good job helping him win election to the New Castle County Council. The campaign eventually became a family project. Owens says,

> I was the campaign manager because I was the only one who took him seriously. My mom was the coffee chairman, my brother Jimmy Biden was the finance chair, my brother Frankie Biden was the volunteer coordinator.[38]

To win women voters, Biden's mother hosted get-togethers at homes of supporters and served coffee and doughnuts. Biden Sr. campaigned with Biden at rallies. But when he accompanied his son, some people mistakenly thought he was the candidate because he was older and more distinguished looking than his son. Biden had little money to spend for radio or television ads to introduce himself to voters, but he got extensive free news media coverage because reporters were intrigued and impressed with the political newcomer. His campaign also attracted many young volunteers who distributed campaign literature to houses throughout the state; some of them were students of Neilia and Valerie, who were both teachers. Biden himself campaigned tirelessly giving speeches and visiting elected officials in communities across Delaware to let them know that he would work for their interests if he was elected.

Unexpected Victory

During the summer, Biden trailed Boggs by thirty percentage points in election polls. But in the final months of the campaign, his stands on issues and increased name recognition began to help him pull even with his opponent. Biden supported civil rights for African Americans, improved health care, protection for the environment, and more mass-transit systems. His most powerful issue was the Vietnam War. He thought the United States should withdraw its troops, a view many people held then about the increasingly divisive war. His popularity gradually rose through September and October and by Election Day the race was considered a dead heat.

On November 7, 1972, Biden defeated Boggs by 3,162 votes out of 230,000 cast. Biden's triumph would soon be followed by a horrible tragedy.

In the weeks after his election, Biden regularly traveled to Washington, D.C., to prepare to become a senator when his term began on January 3, 1973. Biden was in the nation's capital on December 18, 1972, interviewing people for positions with his Senate staff when his brother James called and asked to speak to Valerie. When Biden's sister got off the telephone, she told him they had to go home immediately because his wife and children had been an accident. Valerie told him the accident was

Senator-elect Joe Biden and wife Neilia cut his 30th birthday cake at a party on November 20, 1972. Upon his birthday, Biden fulfilled the constitutional requirement of senators being 30 years of age when they take office.

A Very Young Senator

When Joe Biden was sworn in as a U.S. senator on January 3, 1973, he was the sixth youngest person to ever become a senator. The U.S. Constitution requires members of the U.S. Senate to be at least thirty years old to serve. Biden was only twenty-nine when he was elected on November 7, 1972, but he turned thirty just thirteen days later, and he was thirty years, one month, and fourteen days old when he took office. Ironically, the youngest person ever elected a senator should never have been allowed to run for that office. On November 16, 1818, John Henry Eaton of Tennessee was sworn in as a senator even though he was only twenty-eight years old. Apparently no one had ever checked to see how old he was, and Eaton was allowed to serve. Biden was so young looking that he sometimes had trouble with Capitol security guards who did not recognize him and had trouble believing he was actually a senator. His youth, however, did not stop Biden from getting to sit at a historic desk in the Senate chamber. The drawer of the desk he was assigned bore the name of John F. Kennedy, a Massachusetts senator who became president and who was one of Biden's political heroes. Senators began putting their names in the drawers around 1900 and the tradition continues today.

not serious but Biden immediately felt something terrible had happened and his response was "she's dead, isn't she?"[39]

Grief and Despair

Biden flew home, and when he arrived at Wilmington General Hospital, doctors told him the terrible news. Neilia and his infant daughter, Naomi Christina, were dead. He also learned that his sons had been critically injured. Three-year-old Beau had broken bones, and two-year-old Robert had head injuries. Neilia had been out Christmas shopping with the children when her car collided with a tractor-trailer truck.

Only weeks after the joy of being elected to the Senate, Biden was thrown into despair. His mother tried to comfort him by telling him, "Joey, God sends no cross that you cannot bear."[40] But for Biden, the burden was nearly too much for him to bear. Biden was so full of grief and anger that even his religion, which had always meant so much to him, could not console him. "I felt God had played a horrible trick on me, and I was angry,"[41] Biden writes. He thought about killing himself by jumping off a bridge. He never did attempt suicide, but Biden, a nondrinker, began drinking to numb his emotions. He says,

> I'd get up in the middle of the night, go out and take out a bottle of Scotch and I'd sit at the table and I'd try to make myself just lose it. The hardest part is you feel guilty when you realize you want to live. If the love was as great and as profound as you believed it to be, why would you still want to live?[42]

Shortly after Biden's election, his wife Neilia and infant daughter Naomi Christina died in a car accident.

"Work. Work. Work."

The U.S. Senate is sometimes called the world's most exclusive club because it has only one hundred members, two from each of the nation's fifty states, and because each senator wields so much political power. Despite differences they may have on political issues, many senators become good friends. Biden's fellow senators became like a second family to him and most tried to ease his pain after the death of his wife and daughter in 1972. One senator who Biden had not met before, John McClellan of Arkansas, had some strong advice. Biden recalls the conversation in the following excerpt from *Washingtonian* magazine:

Arkansas senator John McClellan offered a grieving Biden sympathy and advice.

"Oh, you're the guy from Delaware. Lost your wife and kid, huh?" He [McClellan] said it without a hint of sympathy. I felt the urge to smack him across his round pink cheek, but he just kept talking. "Only one thing to do. Bury yourself in work." I couldn't speak, but he could tell I didn't appreciate his advice. "You're mad at me, aren't you, son? But I know what you're going through." Then he told me his own story. He'd lost a wife to spinal meningitis during his first term in the House of Representatives; one son died of the same illness eight years later. He had since lost two more sons. "Work," he told me. "Work. Work. Work."

Quoted in Nancy Doyle Palmer, "Joe Biden: Everyone Calls Me Joe," *Washingtonian*, February 2009, p. 42.

Despite his numbing grief over the deaths of his wife and daughter, Biden knew his first priority was to help his sons recover from their injuries. He moved into their hospital room and stayed with them as much as possible until they were discharged. Biden was scheduled in a few weeks to be sworn in as a senator but he decided to resign because "Delaware can get another senator, but my boys can't get another dad."[43] However, when Biden told Senate Majority Leader Mike Mansfield he wanted to quit, Mansfield pleaded with him not to make a hasty decision. Mansfield called him almost every day to offer him support. He also told Biden that he should keep the job because he had an obligation to all the people who had voted for him. Many other senators, including Hubert Humphrey of Minnesota and Ted Kennedy of Massachusetts, also rallied around the young man they hoped would join them in the Senate.

Mansfield finally convinced Biden to keep the job by telling him that Biden could try it for six months and then quit if he thought it was the right thing to do for his family. Biden agreed and on January 3, 1973, he took the oath of office at the bedside of his sons, who were still hospitalized.

A New Life

Biden felt more like an observer than a participant when he became a senator because he was still more concerned about his sons than his job. "My future was telescoped into putting one foot in front of the other … Washington, politics, the Senate had no hold on me,"[44] he says. Even though family members were helping to care for Beau and Robert—his sister, Valerie, quit working and moved into Biden's home to help—he still felt he needed to be home as much as possible to be with them. So the freshman senator began commuting to work from Wilmington to Washington, D.C., usually by train but sometimes by plane, so that his sons would have daily contact with their only parent. Biden says,

> Being a single parent is hard. I couldn't afford to have someone take care of my kids. But I had my mother, my brothers, my sister. I had a family that just took care of me. [And] my being home every day was sort of the touchstone for me.[45]

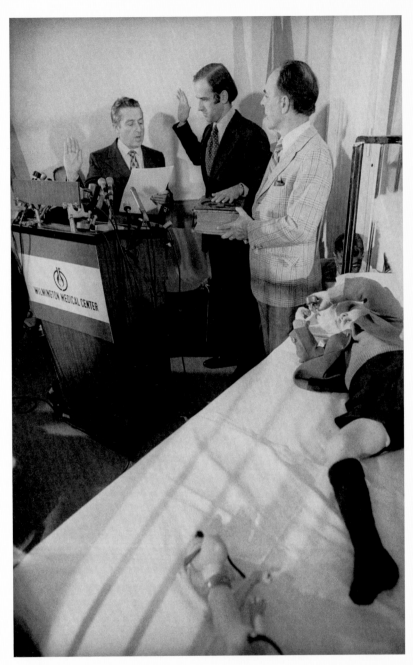

Biden took the oath of office for his U.S. Senate seat in the hospital at the bedside of his sons Beau, right, and Robert, who were recovering from the car accident.

Biden missed his wife so much that he would sometimes wear her high school class ring. When Biden did that, his Senate staff members knew he was especially troubled about the accident that still haunted him. But as time passed, Biden began coping with life again. He credits his parents and family members, especially Valerie, who he has always considered his closest friend, with helping him get through the difficult period in his life. And his brother Frank helped Biden meet his second wife, who turned his life around.

In March 1975, Frank told Joe about a woman he thought would be good company for him. He even gave Joe her telephone number. Biden called Jill Jacobs and asked her out on a date. When they met, Biden was shocked to discover that she was the blond woman he had seen on posters advertising a local park in Wilmington. Biden had been impressed by her beauty when he saw the posters, and he liked her immediately on their first date. For her part, Jacobs knew Biden was a senator but she was not interested in politics. However, she knew Biden's personal story and was touched by his tragedy.

The two began dating and fell in love. Biden credits his relationship with Jacobs with finally pulling him out of his postaccident depression and making him happy again: "She gave me back my life; she made me start to think my family might be whole again. She was beautiful, sure, humble and confident, and she had a rock-ribbed strength."[46] Biden's sons also liked Jacobs. Two years after Biden met her, his sons approached him and said, "We've been thinking about it. And we think it's time that we marry Jill."[47]

Biden proposed to Jacobs and they were married on June 17, 1977. Beau and Robert were on the altar during the wedding ceremony at the United Nations Chapel in New York. The night of the wedding, the newly married couple, Beau, and Robert went to see the Broadway play *Annie*.

"I'm Happy You're Back"

Jacobs quit her job as a high school teacher to raise Beau and Robert so that Biden could concentrate on his Senate duties. The Biden family also grew by one on June 8, 1981, when their daughter Ashley Blazer was born. When Biden returned to work and entered the Capitol building, a Capitol police officer stopped him and asked, "Senator Biden, do you remember me? I'm the fellow that stopped you ten years ago." When Biden toured the Capitol while still a college student, he had accidentally wandered into the Senate chamber and that same officer had guided him away from the restricted area. Biden remembered the incident and said hello. The officer then said, "I'm retiring tomorrow. But, Senator, welcome. I'm happy you're back."[48]

Chapter 4

Political Successes
and Failures

Joe Biden admits he did not devote himself wholeheartedly to his job as a U.S. senator when he was elected in 1972. "The first several years," Biden told one reporter, "I did my job and went home. Period. I didn't want to be there. I did what my dear father would call a workmanlike job."[49] Biden did not work very hard because he was more concerned about raising his sons after their mother died.

Despite his devotion to his sons, Biden was more than adequate in fulfilling his Senate duties. Biden went to work every day, studied the issues, and gradually won the admiration of his colleagues. Biden was assigned to the Senate committees on foreign relations and on the judiciary. His work on these two prestigious committees helped establish Biden as a serious lawmaker. He later served as chairman of both committees—judiciary from 1987 until 1995 and foreign relations from June 2001 through 2003.

Biden also studied how the Senate operated so he could become an effective legislator. Biden received solid advice from prominent senators like Mike Mansfield of Montana, who was Senate majority leader longer than anyone else (1961 to 1977). Mansfield told Biden he could criticize other lawmakers on political issues but he should not attack them personally: "Your job here is to find the good things in your colleagues and not focus on the bad. And, Joe, never attack another man's motive, because you don't know his motive."[50] That advice helped Biden learn

In the Senate, Biden (left) was assigned to the Foreign Relations Committee. He later became its chairman.

how to disagree with other senators on political issues without making enemies.

In the first two years of his first six-year Senate term, Biden performed so well that *Time* magazine in 1974 included him among two hundred young people it predicted would have an impact on the nation's future. According to the magazine,

> Biden admits to being compulsively ambitious. An active proponent of environmental and consumer-protection legislation, he has criticized the Senate for failing to stand up to the Executive Branch and has called for greater accountability on the part of Government decision makers "so I will know whom to crucify."[51]

Biden's position on issues, like making the federal government accountable for how much it spent on programs and whether it spent the funds wisely, helped him be reelected to new terms in 1978, 1984, 1990, 1996, 2002, and 2008, usually by commanding margins of 60 percent of the votes cast. And the longer Biden served in the Senate, the greater his political accomplishments became.

The Foreign Relations Committee

The U.S. Senate Committee on Foreign Relations deals with the United States' relations with other countries, and Biden worked hard to become an expert on foreign policy matters. One issue Biden championed was to have the United States and the Soviet Union reduce their numbers of nuclear weapons to lessen the threat of a nuclear war that could destroy the world.

On June 18, 1979, President Jimmy Carter and Soviet leader Leonid Brezhnev signed a Strategic Arms Limitation Treaty (SALT) to substantially reduce nuclear weapons. When the Senate seemed ready to reject the treaty, Biden acted to save it. He met with Soviet foreign minister Andrey Gromyko and achieved changes in treaty language that won more Senate support for the treaty. However, the Senate eventually refused to ratify the treaty after the Soviet Union invaded Afghanistan in December 1979. Biden's

U.S. president Jimmy Carter, left, and Soviet leader Leonid Brezhnev, right, shake hands in 1979 after signing the SALT treaty. Biden worked hard to save the treaty from rejection in the Senate.

work on SALT increased his political stature because he obtained Soviet concessions President Carter had not been able to win.

After Ronald Reagan was elected president in 1980, Biden became a fierce critic of Reagan's hostile attitude toward the Soviet Union because he believed it kept the two nations from talking and settling their differences. Biden criticized what he called "the dangerous and simplistic Reagan obsession with the 'Soviet menace' that has given us one of the most reckless and misguided foreign policy agendas in the history of modern statecraft."[52]

The Judiciary Committee

The U.S. Senate Committee on the Judiciary deals with issues important to voters, like drug policy, crime prevention, and civil liberties. One of Biden's major accomplishments on the committee came in 1984 when he led the fight to pass the Comprehensive Crime Control Act. He was praised for winning concessions in the law to protect civil liberties for people charged with crimes. While working on such bills, Biden became a close ally of labor unions, civil rights leaders, and women's groups. One of the hardest issues for Biden was abortion. As a Roman Catholic, Biden believes abortion is wrong. But because he does not think he has the right to impose his view on other people, Biden voted to uphold federal law allowing abortions.

Biden worked hard and was almost always well prepared for his Senate duties. But during one judiciary committee hearing, Biden was explaining an amendment he had made to a bill when a member of his staff handed him a copy of his proposal. Biden read it and realized that he had just misspoken about the amendment. Biden admitted to fellow lawmakers: "Obviously, I don't know what the hell I'm talking about."[53] His sense of humor allowed Biden to make fun of himself and it made him popular with other senators. His engaging personality, position on important issues, and ability as a rousing speaker also made him well-known across the nation. In fact, Biden became so popular that he began thinking again about his dream to become president.

Running for President

Biden considered running for president in 1984 but decided not to because he thought he needed more experience. As the 1988 election approached, Biden not only believed he was qualified to be president but that he also had a chance to win. For one thing, Vice President George H.W. Bush, the Republican nominee, was not considered to be a strong candidate. And the race for the Democratic presidential nomination was wide open. There was no obvious front-runner.

On June 9, 1987, Biden announced his candidacy and confidently told reporters, "I'm going to win this thing. I really am. I just know it. I can feel it in my fingertips."[54] Not many people were so sure Biden would be victorious because he had a lot of competition. Biden was one of seven Democratic candidates the news media dubbed the "Seven Dwarfs" because none of them seemed any more imposing than the others.

Most of the candidates seemed bland and uninteresting compared to Biden, who stood out because he was such a fiery and

Senator Biden and his wife Jill wade through a crowd as Biden campaigns for the presidency in 1987. Although he later withdrew from the race, Biden stood out as a great speaker.

eloquent speaker. Early in the campaign, Biden delivered a rousing speech to Democrats in Des Moines, Iowa. David Nagle, a former chairman of the Iowa Democratic Party, praised Biden's eloquence, saying, "It was as close to a 10 as a guy can do."[55]

Allegations of Plagiarism

During the 1988 presidential election, Joe Biden was accused of plagiarizing a speech by British Labor Party leader Neil Kinnock. Biden borrowed the material because he and Kinnock had a similar family history—both were from poor families, became educated, and were elected to high office. Biden credited Kinnock for material he used in other speeches but in a speech he gave in Iowa he forgot. The resulting allegation that he stole Kinnock's speech forced him to withdraw from the race. The following excerpt from *Esquire* magazine explains how closely Biden copied Kinnock's speech and how he sometimes misrepresented his family history to coincide with that of Kinnock.

The local [Iowa] reporters didn't think much about it because they'd heard him credit Kinnock before. [Then reporter] Maureen Dowd broke the story in the *New York Times*. Where Kinnock spoke of ancestors who "could sing and play and write poetry," Biden cited ancestors who "read poetry and wrote poetry and taught me how to sing." Where Kinnock said they worked eight hours underground and came up to play football, Biden said his ancestors worked twelve hours in the coal mines and came up to play football. But there weren't any poets or coal miners in Biden's family. He lifted [Kinnock's] speech complete with "phrases, gestures, and lyrical Welsh syntax intact." The next day, NBC [television] ran the two speeches on a split screen. Dowd was right. Biden even shook his fist at the exact moment Kinnock shook his fist.

John H. Richardson, "Joe," *Esquire*, February 2009, p. 80.

However, Biden's speeches were sometimes too long because he loved to talk. While Biden was addressing Democrats in Orlando, Florida, in August 1987, an aide passed him a note. Biden told the audience, "He's telling me to shut up."[56] The note was not actually a warning to stop talking, and the Democrats laughed because they knew Biden was mocking his reputation for long-windedness.

In August 1987, Biden was trailing Massachusetts governor Michael Dukakis and Indiana senator Richard Gephardt in political polls. But on August 23 Biden delivered a speech at the Iowa State Fair that was so effective that he soon tied them for the lead in the primary race. That speech, however, would prove to be a big political blunder.

A Charge of Plagiarism

Biden's speech at the Iowa State Fair included elements of a campaign speech once given by British political leader Neil Kinnock. Biden used Kinnock's words because Kinnock's life mirrored his own as both men rose from humble beginnings to political power. Although Biden had credited Kinnock in past speeches, he forgot to do that in Iowa. Unfortunately, the Dukakis campaign videotaped the speech, gave it to the news media, and claimed that Biden plagiarized Kinnock's words.

The video was shown repeatedly on television, and the question of Biden's honesty became more explosive when the media reported that he had been accused of plagiarism while attending law school. His failure to credit Kinnock in one speech seemed to be a harmless mistake, and Biden was stunned by the uproar it created. Claiming he was "frustrated" and "angry as hell," Biden stated, "It's so easy to make things look like there's something sinister about them. I don't understand all this."[57] The controversy worsened when the media claimed that Biden had also misrepresented his law school academic record in an appearance in New Hampshire.

The question of a candidate's honesty was especially sensitive at this time because of Colorado senator Gary Hart, who had been the front-runner for the Democratic nomination until reporters discovered he had lied about having an extramarital affair. Hart then lost so much support that that he had to quit the race. As Biden's support eroded and campaign contributions faltered, Biden realized he could not win, even though he did not believe he had done anything wrong. He withdrew from the race on September 23, 1987, saying, "I have only myself to be angry with."[58]

The humiliating end to Biden's campaign months before the first primary was a big and painful political failure. But his roller-coaster career soon took another swing upward when he returned to Washington, D.C.

The Bork Nomination

On January 6, 1987, Biden became chairman of the judiciary committee. On September 15, while his campaign was crumbling, Biden began presiding over hearings on federal judge Robert Bork's nomination to the U.S. Supreme Court. The hearings were contentious

Senate Judiciary Chairman Biden, left, speaks with Supreme Court nominee Robert Bork, center, in 1987.

because Bork, a conservative, would replace Justice Lewis Powell, a moderate who had retired. Before the hearings began, Biden stated that he would question Bork on his past decisions as a judge because they had been politically motivated and opposed past Supreme Court decisions on issues such as abortion, civil rights, and freedom of expression. In August Biden said,

> We can be certain, if Judge Bork has meant what he has written for the past 30 years, that had he been [Supreme Court]

A Frightening Experience

For almost a year, Joe Biden had been ignoring persistent, painful headaches because he thought they were due to stress and fatigue. But on February 10, 1988, after Biden spoke to college students in Rochester, New York, he had a headache that was so bad he knew he was very sick. After returning home, he saw a doctor and was diagnosed with a brain aneurysm. According to a *Washington Post* newspaper story,

> after his speech, [Biden] returned to the hotel and was in the midst of deciding whether to order a pizza when the pain hit. "I was sitting on the bed fully clothed and I collapsed and I don't know if I got knocked out for a second or a minute. There was horrible pain. Let me put it this way: It was a pain I had never experienced before. I didn't know what the hell was happening. I got up after the pain and realized I could still move, had control of my faculties. I could use my hands and I could see. I even tried to speak, and realized I could speak. I knew I wasn't having a heart attack because I wouldn't be able to do those things. I didn't know what the devil it was but I knew it was real serious at this point.

Lois Romano, "The Second Life of Joe Biden; After Campaign Disaster and a Near-Fatal Illness, a Calmer, More Resolute Senator," *Washington Post*, January 12, 1989.

Justice Bork during the past 30 years and had his view prevailed, America would be a fundamentally different place than it is today.[59]

Biden and many other liberal senators, like Ted Kennedy, believed Bork's conservative social and judicial views would lead him to limit rights, such as a woman's right to have an abortion. Biden believed it was fair to evaluate high court nominees on their political ideology as well as their judicial qualifications. But despite his concerns over Bork's conservative views, Biden was praised by both Democrats and Republicans for being fair to Bork during three weeks of hearings. When the Senate rejected Bork by a vote of 58–42 on October 23, it was vindication for Biden's belief that Bork was not suited to be a justice.

The accolades Biden received and the positive news stories that were published about his handling of the Bork nomination eased the sting of his presidential campaign failure. It also made Biden realize that his political career was not over; he had been able to return to Washington and do his job well. His work was making a difference in the government and in the lives of everyday people. But soon, Biden would face another challenge that would threaten his career and his life.

A Brush with Death

Biden began experiencing frequent and painful headaches in the spring of 1987 while campaigning for president in New Hampshire. Biden believed the headaches were caused by stress and fatigue due to his campaign, and he did not see a doctor about them. Although the headaches continued and became more painful, Biden did nothing except take aspirin to alleviate the pain. On February 10, 1988, Biden gave a speech at Rochester University in New York. In his hotel room that night, Biden suffered the most painful headache he had ever experienced, one so strong that he lost consciousness. A shaky Biden managed to fly home to Wilmington the next day but was immediately hospitalized.

Biden leaves Bethesda Hospital in March 1988 after recovering from surgery as a result of a brain aneurysm.

Doctors discovered that Biden had a brain aneurysm, an abnormality in a blood vessel in his brain that could kill or incapacitate him. Biden says, "They were certain it had bled and something had to be done quickly. A local priest came in and I knew they knew it was serious when I was given the last rites."[60] Last rites

A Very Important Public Appearance

During his long convalescence after suffering a brain aneurysm in February 1988, Joe Biden always believed that he would be able to recover and resume being a U.S. senator. But some people thought his medical problems had been so severe that he would not be able to continue serving in the Senate. That is why his first major public appearance since falling ill was so important to him. He chose to speak at the annual Sussex County Jamboree in Delaware in August 1988. In the following excerpt, *Time* magazine describes Biden's arrival at the event:

> The Senator is swamped by friends and the curious, all straining to get a glimpse of the man who vanished from sight seven months ago. In a blazer and an open-neck shirt that reveals a tiny scar, he looks like the healthiest person here, trim, energetic and tan. He makes his way to a picnic bench, where he waits his turn to speak at what he calls the "most important event in my public life." Biden is listening as Senate Candidate Sam Beard introduces him, recalling the night he got a call from the state police accompanying Biden's ambulance saying "We don't think he's going to make it." Biden whispers to his wife Jill, "Neither did I." He takes her onto the podium with him, along with his kids, although he says he "usually does not go in for that type of stuff."

Margaret Carlson, "Biden Is Also Reborn," *Time*, September 12, 1988, www.time.com/time/magazine/article/0,9171,968383-1,00.html.

is the blessing a Roman Catholic priest gives to someone who is near death.

Biden was flown to Walter Reed Army Medical Center in Washington, D.C., and on February 12 had a nine-hour operation to fix the aneurysm. His recovery was long and painful. He needed two more surgeries in the next few months, one to correct a second, smaller aneurysm and the other to fix an embolism—an obstructed blood vessel—in his lung. Biden did not return to his Senate duties until September, which allowed him to spend more time with his wife, who had started teaching again, and his two sons and daughter.

As with many people who have had a brush with death, Biden had a new appreciation for just being alive. Biden calls his recovery "my second chance in life" and gratefully admits, "It just wasn't my time. Thank God, because it saved my life. I'm alive. I'm well. My family is happy. I do something I love."[61] When Biden finally returned to the Senate, he also had a new attitude toward his work and political future. When reporters asked what he was going to do he said, "I don't know if I will ever run for president again, but if I do, the best way to prepare for it is [to] do my job, to learn more about the issues I'm dealing with, to demonstrate the staying power and the seriousness a lot of you [reporters] doubted that I have."[62]

And that is exactly what Biden did for the next two decades before deciding to run for president a second time.

Chapter 5

The 2008 Presidential Campaign

In the years following his 1988 presidential campaign failure, Joe Biden dedicated himself to his work. As chairman of the judiciary committee, Biden was responsible for the passage of two important crime bills in 1994—the Violent Crime Control and Law Enforcement Act and the landmark Violence Against Women Act. The first bill, also known as the Biden Crime Bill, provides billions of dollars in funding for new police officers, prisons, and crime-prevention programs. The second measure funds new efforts to combat domestic violence and deal with gender-based crimes, and Biden considers passage of that bill one of his greatest legislative accomplishments. Biden also continued to be one of the foreign relations committee's most influential members. In 1998 the political journal *Congressional Quarterly* named Biden as one of twelve congressmen who had made a difference on important global issues, such as his work to combat religious persecution around the world.

On the morning of September 11, 2001, Biden was riding the train into Washington, D.C., when terrorists crashed planes into the World Trade Center in New York, the Pentagon in Virginia, and a field in Pennsylvania. Jill called Biden while he was on the train and told him about the attacks. Biden saw the smoke rising from the Pentagon when he got off the train in Washington. He writes,

> The planes hit while I was on the train from Wilmington to Washington, and when I came out of Union Station

As he walked to the U.S Capitol on September 11, 2001, Biden could see smoke rising from the Pentagon, pictured, which was one of several targets in a terrorist attack.

that morning, I could see a haze of smoke rising from the Pentagon across the Potomac. It was a morning of surreal stillness. There was almost no breeze. It was so quiet, I could hear myself breathe as I walked toward the Capitol.[63]

The terrorist attacks killed nearly three thousand people. They led the United States to invade Afghanistan and Iraq and to Biden's decision to run again for president.

The Iraq War

Because of his expertise on foreign affairs, Biden was not surprised by the attacks. In fact in a strange twist of fate, Biden only one day earlier had warned of the possibility of such a terrorist attack. In a speech at the National Press Club in Washington, D.C., Biden claimed the United States was not taking enough steps to protect itself from terrorists. He said, "[The] real threat comes to this country in the hold of a ship, the belly of a plane, or smuggled into a city in the middle of the night in a vial in a backpack."[64] His prediction that terrorist violence could harm the United States came true the next day.

Biden's comments on September 10 had been aimed at President George W. Bush, who he claimed was incompetent in dealing with other countries and was ignoring such threats against the United States. Despite his lack of faith in Bush's foreign policies, Biden supported the president's decision to invade Afghanistan on October 7, 2001, because that country was sheltering Osama bin Laden, the leader of the terrorist group al Qaeda and the person who organized the attack on the United States. But Biden did not support Bush a year later when Bush began calling for an invasion of Iraq.

Bush argued it was proper to use military force against Iraq because Saddam Hussein, Iraq's dictator, supported al Qaeda and had access to weapons of mass destruction, weapons that can kill large numbers of people and destroy buildings, roads, and property. Biden argued that even if the allegations were true—both claims were later proven false—it would be better to use diplomacy and economic penalties against Iraq to deal with those situations. Biden and Indiana senator Richard G. Lugar, the top Republican on the foreign relations committee, drafted a resolution to use those methods instead of military force. But Congress rejected their proposal and after weeks of debate, it passed the Joint Resolution to Authorize the Use of United States Armed Forces Against Iraq on October 11, 2002. The House of Representatives approved the measure 296–133, and the Senate approved it 77–23.

Biden voted for the bill but only because he still hoped Bush would only use force as a last resort; the bill explicitly urged the president to try to settle the conflict peacefully before resorting to war. Several years later in explaining his vote, Biden claimed, "Despite the doubts I heard [about Iraq having weapons of mass destruction], I voted to give the president the authority to avoid a war [and not necessarily start one]."[65] Bush, however, was eager to score another military victory like the one over Afghanistan. Thus, Biden and other senators who had urged diplomacy to end the confrontation were disappointed when the United States and its allies, like Great Britain, invaded Iraq on March 20, 2003.

Biden, far right, attends an October 2002 speech by President George W. Bush, left, on the use of force in Iraq.

Running for President Again

U.S. forces quickly defeated Iraq's army and captured Hussein. But after what appeared to be an easy victory, U.S. forces became bogged down in a prolonged fight against Iraqi insurgents— Iraqis who resented the presence of U. S. forces in Iraq and wanted them to leave. Biden had warned against U.S. intervention in Iraq. He said, "It would be a tragedy if we removed a tyrant [dictator Saddam Hussein] in Iraq only to leave chaos in its wake."[66] And as more U.S. soldiers died and Iraq appeared headed for civil war instead of a peaceful transition to democracy, the American public grew increasingly unhappy with the war.

In 2004 Bush narrowly won reelection against Democratic senator John Kerry. Despite his opposition to Bush policies on Iraq and other issues, Biden had not run because he believed Kerry would win. But Biden decided to run in 2008 because he believed he had the foreign policy expertise the next president would need to deal with problems in the Middle East and other parts of the world. In July 2006 he told *Time* magazine, "The other guys are allegedly making up their minds. I've been around too long to be coy. My objective is to run."[67]

Biden formally announced his candidacy on July 31, 2007. Eventually eight Democratic candidates, including Biden, entered the race. The first primary was in Iowa in January 2008. Knowing this, Biden had spent two weeks wooing voters there in August 2006. Biden also held fundraisers around the country in August 2006 and spoke to the National Association for the Advancement of Colored People (NAACP) in South Carolina to get an early start on his rivals.

In his campaign stops, Biden boasted about his foreign policy experience. At the University of Iowa he claimed, "I've forgotten more about these issues than most of these guys who are running know."[68] His foreign policy experience helped Biden become a leading candidate for the nomination because in addition to the ongoing Iraq War, the United States also faced serious problems with Russia, Iran, and Korea. Biden's energetic speaking style captivated audiences, and he was able to raise millions of dollars for his campaign. But at one campaign appearance in Iowa, Biden admitted, "I'm not a superstar. People say they like me, people tell me they think I'd be a good president but that they just don't think I can win."[69] Unfortunately for Biden, they were right.

Bowing out Again

Despite Biden's experience and personal appeal, his candidacy never caught fire. The main problem was that Senators Hillary Clinton of New York and Barack Obama of Illinois were attracting almost all the media attention and support of other Democrats because their candidacies were historic. Clinton was the first woman and Obama was the first African American who had a good chance of being elected president. Clinton, whose husband, Bill, had been president from 1993 to 2001, was the front-runner throughout 2007. Obama was a strong second with Biden and several other candidates badly trailing the two front-runners.

Biden also had himself to blame for making statements that damaged his candidacy. In July 2007 while discussing how successful immigrants from India had been in running small businesses in Delaware, he said, "You cannot go to a 7-Eleven or a Dunkin' Donuts unless you have a slight Indian accent. I'm not joking."[70] And in August Biden tried to explain why Obama was a strong candidate. He said, "I mean, you got the first mainstream African-American who is articulate and bright and clean and a nice-looking guy, I mean, that's a storybook, man."[71] Biden had meant for his remarks to be complimentary to minorities but many people were offended. Biden was accused of being racially insensitive, a charge that hurt him because he had a long record of fighting for minority rights.

During 2007, Biden appeared in televised debates with the other Democratic candidates. In the August 19 debate, George Stephanopoulos of ABC News asked Biden about a comment he had made about Obama:

STEPHANOPOULOS: You were asked: Is he ready? You said, "I think he can be ready, but right now I don't believe he is. The presidency is not something that lends itself to on-the-job training."

BIDEN: I think I stand by the statement.[72]

Critics said Biden handled himself well in the debates. They praised his honesty in commenting on Obama's political weakness

Well Suited for the Job

When Barack Obama needed to choose a vice presidential running mate, he wanted someone who could not only help him win the election but who also had the expertise to advise him and help him govern the nation after he was elected. Vermont senator Patrick Leahy was one of the people who helped Obama choose a vice president. In the following excerpt from *Washingtonian* magazine, Leahy explains why Biden is well suited to be Obama's vice president:

I was with the vice-presidential selection committee. I told Barack Obama I saw three criteria. First and most obvious, God forbid if something happens to you, you have to have somebody who can take over on a second's notice. Second, you've got to have somebody who can work with the House and Senate and get your programs through. In my experience only two vice presidents did that role really well: George H.W. Bush and [Walter] Mondale. And third, when you think you're doing everything right and you screw up, you gotta have one person come in, close the door, and say, "I think you screwed up and here's why," and you know you will never read about it in the press. And Joe Biden would fit all three of these criteria.

Quoted in Nancy Doyle Palmer, "Joe Biden: Everyone Calls Me Joe," *Washingtonian*, February 1, 2009, www.washingtonian.com/articles/people/11118.html.

Barack Obama, right, wanted a vice president who had the expertise to help him govern the nation. He found that expertise in Joe Biden.

that he had only been a senator for two years. But Biden struggled to attract voters because Clinton and Obama got most of the media attention and were able to raise much more money than Biden did.

On January 3, 2008, Obama won the Iowa primary with 34.9 percent of the vote in a stunning upset over Clinton. After Biden finished fifth with less than 1 percent of the vote, he quit the race.

In an emotional farewell address, Biden told campaign workers, "There is nothing sad about tonight. So many of you have sacrificed for me, and I am so indebted to you. I feel no regret."[73] After another premature end to a presidential campaign, Biden decided to run for a seventh term in the Senate.

Obama Chooses Biden

When Clinton won the New Hampshire primary five days later, the race became a two-way battle between her and Obama. Both candidates tried to win Biden's support, but he remained neutral. Biden even talked to both candidates regularly to offer his views on issues and campaign strategy. He did that because he liked and respected both Clinton and Obama and, in turn, both trusted him.

When Obama finally won the Democratic nomination in June 2008, he had to pick a vice presidential candidate. Obama, after considering many political figures, narrowed his final list of potential running mates to Biden, Indiana senator Evan Bayh, and Virginia governor Tim Kaine. Obama wanted a running mate who would strengthen the Democratic ticket's appeal to working-class voters and labor unions. And because Obama was young and relatively inexperienced, especially in foreign affairs, a candidate with years of experience dealing with those issues would also help him win voters.

Biden met secretly with Obama in August in Minneapolis, Minnesota. They talked for three hours, about the campaign and about how they would work together if Obama chose him as vice president and they were elected. A few days later, Obama offered Biden the job and Biden accepted. On August 23, the Obama campaign announced his choice to supporters throughout the nation via e-mails and text messages. The announcement read, "Barack has chosen Senator Joe Biden to be our VP nominee. Spread the word!"[74] Obama's choice of Biden was widely praised. David Axelrod, Obama's senior campaign adviser, explains, "Mostly, I think what attracted Senator Obama was Biden's wisdom. And not the kind of wisdom you get in Washington, D.C., but the kind of wisdom you get when you overcome adversity, tragedy in your life as he has."[75]

Joe and Jill Biden follow Barack and Michelle Obama after greeting the crowd at the 2008 Democratic National Convention.

Joe Biden's
Convention Speech

Senator Joe Biden accepted the Democratic Party nomination for vice president on August 27, 2008, in a speech at the Democratic National Convention. In his speech, Biden claimed President George W. Bush's foreign policy had hurt the nation and that Republican presidential nominee John McCain would continue many of Bush's policies if elected. Biden said,

> [Today] our country is less secure and more isolated than at any time in recent history. The Bush-McCain foreign policy has dug us into a very deep hole with very few friends to help us climb out. For the last seven years, [the Bush] administration has failed to face the biggest forces shaping this century: the emergence of Russia, China and India as great powers; the spread of lethal weapons; the shortage of secure supplies of energy, food and water; the challenge of climate change; and the resurgence of fundamentalism in Afghanistan and Pakistan, the real central front against terrorism. In recent days, we've once again seen the consequences of this neglect with Russia's challenge to the free and democratic country of Georgia [Russian troops invaded part of Georgia]. Barack Obama and I will end this neglect. We will hold Russia accountable for its actions, and we'll help the people of Georgia rebuild. I've been on the ground in Georgia, Iraq, Pakistan and Afghanistan, and I can tell you in no uncertain terms: this administration's policy has been an abject failure. America cannot afford four more years of this.

Joe Biden, speech, Democratic National Convention, Denver, CO, August 27, 2008, www.foxnews.com/politics/elections/2008/08/27/raw-data-transcript-of-joe-bidens-speech-at-democratic-convention.

Four days later on August 27, Biden accepted the nomination in a nationally televised speech at the Democratic National Convention in Denver, Colorado. He said simply, "Since I've never been called a man of few words, let me say this simply as I can: Yes. Yes, I accept your nomination to run and serve with Barack Obama, the next president of the United States of America."[76] His acceptance was greeted with thunderous applause and chants of "Joe, Joe" by thousands of Democratic delegates.

Campaigning as Vice President

One of Biden's first tasks when he began campaigning for vice president was to respond to a Republican advertisement that resurrected his negative comments about Obama's lack of experience. Biden explains that his criticism had simply been part of his campaign tactics against a candidate he considered very formidable. "I was running against him, man," Biden told one reporter. "What did they expect me to do, lean over and hug him and say, 'Yeah, he was the most experienced? He has plenty of experience?' Hey, man, the only thing I had going was experience."[77]

The negative ad did little damage, and Biden was a valuable asset on the campaign trail. One of his strengths was being able to relate to working-class voters, a factor that became more important as the campaign progressed. The Iraq War had been the top issue when the race began, but during 2008, the worsening U.S. economy became the problem that most concerned voters. Biden, because of his working-class upbringing, understood how much average people were suffering because they had trouble paying their bills, were losing jobs, and were even being evicted from their homes.

In a campaign appearance in October in Rochester, New York, Biden told people not to lose faith. He said, "I've never seen a time in my career when so many Americans have been knocked down. As my father used to say, when you get knocked down, 'GET UP!' So GET UP! Get up and win in New Hampshire! Bring back the promise of this country!"[78] Biden connected with union workers in Akron, Ohio, when he delivered the same message. "I think he expressed what most people feel at the moment. He seems to relate to our pain,"[79] said Bob Wise, a union worker.

Biden proved to be a solid, veteran running mate to the younger Obama and helped win votes for the Democratic ticket.

On October 2 Biden participated in a nationally televised debate against Sarah Palin, the Alaska governor who was the Republican vice presidential nominee. During the debate, Biden claimed that the Republican presidential candidate, John McCain, would govern like the unpopular Bush. He said, "The issue is, how different is John McCain's policy going to be than George Bush's? I haven't heard anything yet."[80] A CBS television poll showed 46 percent of viewers believed Biden won the debate and 21 percent believed Palin won.

The Great Debate

Many people believed Joe Biden was at a disadvantage in his October 2, 2008, debate with Republican vice presidential candidate Sarah Palin because she is a woman. Political analysts said that Biden could not be as rough with Palin in the debate as he could be with a male opponent because he would look like a bully and offend women voters. Analysts also said Palin would be stronger than him in appealing to other women. However, Biden performed ably in the debate by calmly but forcefully answering negative statements Palin made about him and Barack Obama. He also fared well when Palin tried to appeal to women by claiming one of her strengths was that she is a mother who had to worry about her children, including one who has Down syndrome. Biden responded,

> Look, I understand what it's like to be a single parent. When my wife and daughter died and my two sons were gravely injured [in a 1972 auto accident], I understand what it's like as a parent to wonder what it's like if your kid's going to make it. [But] the notion that somehow, because I'm a man, I don't know what it's like to raise two kids alone, I don't know what it's like to have a child you're not sure is going to—is going to make it—I understand.

Joe Biden, vice presidential debate with Sarah Palin, Washington University, St. Louis, MO, October 2, 2008, www.cnn.com/2008/POLITICS/10/02/debate.transcript.

In 2008, Joe Biden debated Alaska governor Sarah Palin, right, and impressed critics who thought he would be at a disadvantage.

A Big Victory

The debate highlighted how influential the vice presidential candidate is in a presidential campaign. Although Palin had seemed a good choice at first because of her fiery oratory and the fact that she is a woman, many voters after several weeks began to realize she did not understand the issues, and her popularity dropped quickly. Biden, however, provided a solid, veteran running mate to the younger Obama and helped win votes for the Democratic ticket.

Obama and Biden achieved a landslide victory on November 4 with 69,456,897 votes to 59,934,814 for McCain and Palin. Biden also won his Senate race with 65 percent of the vote, a post he would have to give up to become vice president. On November 6, Biden returned to Wilmington, Delaware, to a hero's welcome. Riding in a horse-drawn carriage, the vice-president-elect waved to thousands of cheering people lining the streets. "It feels great, it feels great. This is home,"[81] he said.

Chapter 6

Becoming the Vice President of the United States

The final leg of Joe Biden's journey to becoming the forty-seventh vice president of the United States started in Wilmington, Delaware, the same place where his political career had begun nearly four decades earlier. On January 17, 2009, Biden boarded a special train that carried him to Washington, D.C., for his inauguration three days later. Gregg Weaver, an Amtrak conductor Biden knew from his daily commutes, introduced Biden to a crowd of several hundred well-wishers, many of them yelling, "We love you, Joe!" President-elect Barack Obama was already on the train. He told the cheering crowd that Biden would be a good vice president because of what he had learned while growing up. Obama said,

Joe is still the scrappy kid from Scranton [Pennsylvania] whose family moved here—to Wilmington—in search of a new beginning. They'd known their share of hardships, and they would come to know more. They didn't have much money. But Joe [Biden] Senior taught his son about the values that stretched longer than the dollar: the dignity of a hard day's work; the primacy of family; the dream that anyone should be able to make it if they try; and the simple lesson that when we Americans get knocked down, we always—always—get back up on our feet.[82]

It was a stirring tribute to Biden and an emotional pep talk to people in the crowd worried about the future because of problems like the nation's weakened economy. On January 20, Biden took his oath of office on the west steps of the Capitol before nearly 2 million people gathered on the Washington Mall and tens of millions more who were watching on television. Among those proudly watching were Biden's family members, like his ninety-one-year-old mother, Catherine Eugenia "Jean" Biden, and son, Beau Biden, who was home from Iraq where he was serving as a captain with the Delaware National Guard.

The First Hundred Days

New presidents are judged on how they perform in their first hundred days in office. Vice presidents like Joe Biden can be, too. In an interview with correspondent Lesley Stahl on the television show *60 Minutes* on April 26, 2009, President Barack Obama said Biden had been "very valuable" to him in his first few months in office. Obama said he is especially grateful that Biden is not afraid to disagree with him on issues. When Stahl asked if Biden argues with him, Obama said, "Joe Biden has never been shy about speaking his mind. You know, Joe's not afraid to tell me what he thinks. And that's exactly what I need, and exactly what I want." Obama admitted that Biden will also tell him if he is not doing a good enough job explaining his positions on key issues to the public. Obama said, "[If] I'm off message, he's not going to be bashful about saying, 'You know, Mr. President, I think we might want to steer more in that direction.'" Another high-ranking official in the Obama administration who believes Biden has done a good job is Secretary of State Hillary Clinton, who works closely with Biden on foreign policy issues. Clinton told Stahl that she admires Biden's expertise on other nations. Clinton said, "He's been at the highest levels of American foreign policy decision making. And we all listen to him."

Interview by Lesley Stahl, *60 Minutes*, CBS, April 26, 2009, www.cbsnews.com/stories/2009/04/24/60minutes/main4965941.shtml.

A crowd of children in Kosovo cheer Vice President Biden as he arrives in 2008. President Obama said Biden was "very valuable" to him during his first few months in office.

That night Joe and Jill Biden accompanied Barack and Michelle Obama to parties celebrating the inauguration. When it was the Bidens' turn to dance at one ball, the sixty-six-year-old vice president admitted he was nervous about his lack of dancing skills but proud of his beautiful wife. "I may not be able to dance, but I've got a hell of an eye, don't I?"[83] he said with glee. On a more serious note, Biden noted that he was proud to serve as vice president to Obama, the nation's first black president. "Today, we witnessed history," Biden said. "Tomorrow, Barack and I are going to begin to make history."[84]

The Office of Vice President

When Biden was sworn in as vice president, he promised to defend the Constitution, protect the nation against its enemies, and faithfully discharge the duties of the office of vice president.

Vice President Joe Biden works in his office in the White House.

A vice president's most serious duty is to assume the presidency if the president dies, resigns, or is removed from office. This has happened nine times, most recently in 1973 when Vice President Gerald Ford replaced President Richard Nixon after he resigned in disgrace over accusations he tried to conceal illegal actions during his 1972 presidential campaign. The vice president also serves as president of the Senate. That prestigious title, however, holds little power because vice presidents can only vote if a Senate vote is tied on a bill, which rarely happens.

Vice presidents also perform many jobs that are assigned to them by the president. Although many vice presidents have been limited to relatively unimportant or ceremonial tasks, recent Presidents Bill Clinton and George W. Bush have entrusted their vice presidents with major responsibilities. In August 2008 when Obama asked Biden to become his running mate, Biden hesitated before saying yes. Biden did not accept Obama's offer until they met and Obama promised to let Biden counsel him on major issues and play an important role in making daily decisions. Biden described the meeting to a journalist:

> I said to him when he asked me, I said, "Barack, don't ask me unless the reason you're asking me is you're asking me for my judgment. I get to be the last guy in the room when you make every important decision. You're president. Any decision you make, I will back."[85]

Biden began to counsel Obama even before they took office. In the two months between their election and inauguration, Biden advised Obama on who to name to various top government posts and how to handle the most pressing problem the incoming president faced, the faltering economy. True to his working-class roots, Biden told Obama that his plan to strengthen the economy had to include helping individual citizens and not just banks, automakers, and other corporations with financial problems. Biden told Obama:

> If the middle class doesn't grow, America fails, and I just wanted to remind some of the intellectual powerhouses in that meeting [of key Obama advisers] [about that]. It wasn't so much that people weren't consciously aware of the perspective I articulated, but nobody specifically articulated it. I just wanted to make sure, "We're all on the same page, right guys? This has to be done."[86]

Obama counts on Biden as one of his most experienced and closest advisers. When Obama and Biden are both in Washington, D.C., they spend at least three hours each day with each other and sometimes more depending on how many meetings they attend together. Those sessions include morning intelligence and economy briefings as well as meetings with visiting heads of state and other officials. The relationship, according to administration officials, is one in which Biden is a peer of Obama and not a subordinate staffer.

Biden's partnership with Obama in helping govern the nation is a major part of his role as vice president. However, Biden has many more things to do on a daily basis, including important tasks that he handles by himself.

A Very Busy Vice President

The most significant job Obama entrusted Biden with was to oversee spending of the $787 billion of the American Recovery and Reinvestment Act of 2009 that Congress passed just a few weeks after he and Biden took office. The goals of the recovery act are to generate economic activity and invest in long-term economic growth, to create and save jobs, and to maintain a high level of accountability and transparency in spending the money. Biden spent many hours each day in his first few months as vice president meeting with federal, state, and local officials to assess their needs and to decide how the federal government should allocate funds for various projects, such as building highways and schools, improving education, and performing other tasks to strengthen the nation's weakened economy.

Once the money was distributed, Biden continued to meet with officials to make sure it was being spent properly. On April 23, 2009, when the federal government's General Accounting Office issued a report that showed some states were not doing a good job handling the money, Biden immediately promised to help officials correct the problem. He said, "Together, we will work to ensure that every dollar of taxpayer funds under the Recovery Act is moving without delay to the most effective projects and meeting the most urgent needs."[87] Obama also named Biden chairman of the White House Task Force on Middle Class Families. The task force is designed to initiate legislation and programs to help improve life for middle-class, working families, including helping them get better jobs.

Because of Biden's vast foreign affairs experience, Obama chose him to deliver the administration's first major foreign-policy address. Biden spoke to European leaders on February 7 in

Biden Oversees $787 Billion

One of the most important jobs President Barack Obama has given Vice President Joe Biden is to oversee the spending of the $787 billion of the American Recovery and Reinvestment Act of 2009. On March 18, 2009, Biden met with city and county government officials from around the nation. During the meeting, he said,

> We have got to—we have got to get this right. We have got to demonstrate to the American public that we can husband their money and their investments in a way that, in fact, makes sense to them. This can't be government as usual. Every single dollar of this money has to be used—and we're going to make mistakes. We're going to make mistakes. But every single dollar of this money has to be used in a way that is actually producing or keeping jobs from being lost and perceptually make sense [to the public]. So please don't underestimate the consequence of this [because it is] not just for this recovery. We will recover. We will recover. This economy will grow. We will be the leader of the 21st century as we were in the 20th. The question is how long it takes to get there and how painful the journey. But we will.

Joseph R. Biden, remarks to the White House American Recovery and Reinvestment Act Implementation Conference for City and County Governments, March 18, 2009, FDCH Political Transcripts, Item: 32V2245310728.

Munich, Germany. The leaders met to discuss how their countries could work together to strengthen their military security. Biden said, "We believe that international alliances and organizations do not diminish America's power—they help us. America needs the world, just as I believe the world needs America."[88] The sentiment was well-received by European nations who believed that

Biden Rides the Train

After Joe Biden was elected vice president in November 2008, Amtrak workers and riders still treated him like a regular passenger when he made his daily train commute between Delaware and Washington, D.C. In an article in *Esquire* magazine, writer John H. Richardson describes the friendly way Biden is treated on the train:

> He caught the 8:29, his usual morning train, and hurried up the platform to the business car. [Biden said] "And I get to the conductor at the front end and he goes, 'Heeeey, Joey baby!'" Once he got inside the car, it was more of the same. [Biden has] been taking this train for thirty-six years now, eighty minutes each way, and the longtime commuters and train employees know exactly how to treat him. "Hey, Joe, what are you going to do about this economy? We need some help!" [In] Washington, the train discharged him into a long day of formality and meetings, the routine of his stunning new life. But when the day was over, he was back on the seven o'clock for the ride home—and the same thing happened. "Hey, Joey!" When they got off at Wilmington, the lead Secret Service guy came up to Biden. "Can I ask you a question?" he asked. "Sure, anything," Biden answered. "Do people talk to you that way all the time?"

John H. Richardson, "Joe," *Esquire*, February 2009, p. 81.

As vice president, Biden speaks to a crowd about the Middle Class Task Force and its goals for the American people during a struggling economy.

President George W. Bush, Obama's predecessor, had ignored their concerns and done whatever he wanted, including invading Iraq.

Obama also utilized Biden's expertise on other countries by having him work closely with Secretary of State Hillary Clinton, who Obama selected for that prestigious post despite the bitter battle they waged for the Democratic presidential nomination. Biden and Clinton became friends and allies after she was elected a senator from New York in 2000. The vice president and secretary of state have breakfast every Tuesday to discuss the nation's relationships with other countries. And because Biden has known many foreign leaders for years, Obama allows him to telephone leaders of countries, like Colombia and Israel, to talk over mutual concerns or to offer advice on problems those countries are facing. Biden is also valuable to Obama as a contact person with members of Congress. His many years in the Senate made him an expert on how Congress works, and during that time, he also made many friends in both houses of Congress.

Biden throws out the first pitch at a Baltimore Orioles game in 2009. It was one of the more fun tasks of his job as vice president.

Biden also performs many ceremonial duties as vice president. On April 6, 2009, Biden had the honor of throwing out the first pitch when the Baltimore Orioles opened their season against the New York Yankees. Biden practiced ahead of time so he would not embarrass himself in front of baseball fans. After his ceremonial first pitch, Biden told reporters,

> I tell you, my arm's sore. I worked on it [pitching] for two days with my brother in law. I used to be—I used to think I was a pretty good athlete. I was very delighted that as I was walking out and one of the Orioles' employees said, "Hey, Mr. Vice President, great Orioles pitch."[89]

Ted Kaufman was a political adviser to Biden for many years. He was named to succeed Biden when he resigned his Senate seat on January 3, 2009, so he could become vice president. Kaufman believes the fact that Biden is so busy proves that he is doing a good job as vice president. Kaufman says, "His plate is overflowing. By that standard alone, he's been a success."[90]

The honor and success Biden was enjoying as vice president, however, was taking a toll on his private life.

A Public Private Life

In the months between the presidential election and the time Biden took office, most of the news media focused on President-elect Obama in stories about the upcoming inauguration. Biden once said during this period that "ever since the election, nobody pays any attention to me at all."[91] Biden was only kidding. He was actually grateful for a brief respite from the full-scale news coverage he had received during the campaign. Biden also knew that once he became vice president the news media would be even more relentless in reporting his every word and action because of the power and celebrity that go with that position. He also understood that his life would never be the same again because of that new fame.

Most U.S. senators are not well-known to the public except in their home states. This relative anonymity allowed Biden to lead a fairly normal life while he was a senator, including taking the train to work. But because the vice president of the United States is recognized everywhere he goes and he always has the Secret Service with him, it is harder for him to do things average people do, like going to a movie. Despite that, Biden tries to lead a normal life. In an interview after becoming vice president, he said,

> I'm going to do my best not to get trapped in the "bubble." So far it's worked. After Mass I still go to the same coffee shop. It's been more cumbersome, but I know if I work hard at it I can still be available and approachable. The funny thing is in Delaware I've always been Joe, and everyone calls me that. And I hope they always will.[92]

The "bubble" Biden refers to includes not only his new fame but also the extra security from Secret Service agents, who guard the vice president twenty-four hours a day. His Secret Service nickname is "Celtic," a reference to his family's Irish roots. Biden is accompanied everywhere by Secret Service agents—usually just a few but sometimes as many as twenty agents for a big public event—and state and local governments also provide police escorts to protect him when he visits. This heavy security forced Biden to make some changes in his lifestyle. For example, Biden had always enjoyed driving himself around Wilmington, but Secret Service agents now drive him almost everywhere by limousine.

When Biden has to travel long distances, he has the use of military helicopters or a large passenger plane. But "Amtrak Joe" has not abandoned trains completely. Although Secret Service agents hate trains because it is difficult to protect somebody on a train, Biden loves them so much he still travels by train whenever possible. In early March 2009, Biden and a half-dozen top officials took the train from Washington, D.C., to Philadelphia for a session of the White House Task Force on Middle Class Families. His train trips home, however, will be fewer because of his new daily responsibilities, which include early morning news and intelligence briefings and nighttime dinners with foreign officials. However, it is easier for Biden to remain in Washington, D.C., more often because the vice president has an official residence, a mansion built in 1893 located on the grounds of the U. S. Naval Observatory.

It did not take Jill and Joe Biden long to settle into their new home. One of the first things they did was install bunk beds in the home so their grandchildren could stay overnight when they visit. Biden has always been happiest when surrounded by family, and he and Jill expected to see a lot of their three children, Beau, Hunter, and Ashley. Beau, who followed his father's career path into politics, took office in January 2007 as Delaware attorney general; in 2009 he was serving in Iraq with the Delaware National Guard while on a leave of absence from his position with the state. Hunter is a lawyer in Washington, D.C., and Ashley is a social worker in Wilmington.

"We Got It Right"

As long as Biden can be in contact with his family, he is content. Biden is also content being vice president even though he knows he will probably never realize his goal of becoming president because his age would be a disadvantage to any candidacy in the future. Biden had been a powerful and respected senator, but the position of vice president is even more important. When Biden visited Whiteman Air Force Base in St. Louis, Missouri, on March 16, 2009, he joked about how much easier it is to make sure people attend the meetings he schedules. He said, "When I was a United States Senator and a powerful chairman, I'd have to plead. Now I can just call a cabinet meeting. They all show up. (laughs) You know what I mean?"[93]

Biden is also content to be vice president to Obama, the first African American president. Talking about the election, Biden notes that "this is an historic moment. [It's] a new America. It's the reflection of a new America. And I think we got it right. We got it right, the president and vice-president. It's the right order."[94]

Introduction: A Vice President Named Joe

1. Quoted in John H. Richardson, "Joe," *Esquire*, February 2009, p. 78.
2. Quoted in Craig Crawford, "Joe Biden Fights Hard, Talks Harder Bork Hearings Will Put Senator in the Limelight," *Sentinel (Orlando, FL)*, September 6, 1987.
3. Joe Biden, interview by Katie Couric, *CBS Evening News*, September 22, 2008, http://cbs2.com/politics/joe.biden.interview.2.823202.html.
4. Joe Biden, *Promises to Keep: On Life and Politics*, New York: Random House, 2007, p. xxiii.

Chapter 1: Raised in a Loving Family

5. Quoted in Nancy Doyle Palmer, "Joe Biden: Everyone Calls Me Joe," *Washingtonian*, February 2009, p. 40.
6. Quoted in John M. Broder, "Father's Tough Life an Inspiration for Biden," *New York Times*, October 23, 2008, www.nytimes.com/2008/10/24/us/politics/24biden.html?_r=1.
7. Quoted in Crawford, "Joe Biden Fights Hard."
8. Quoted in Biden, *Promises to Keep*, p. 13.
9. Quoted in Borys Krawczeniuk, "Remembering His Roots," *Scranton Times*, August 24, 2008.
10. Quoted in Joe Biden, speech, Democratic National Convention, Denver, CO, August 27, 2008, www.foxnews.com/politics/elections/2008/08/27/raw-data-transcript-of-joe-bidens-speech-at-democratic-convention.
11. Biden, *Promises to Keep*, p. 22.
12. Quoted in Christine Brozyna, "Get to Know Joe Biden: The Delaware Senator Has Overcome Personal Tragedy on His Journey to Washington," ABC News, December 13, 2007, http://abcnews.go.com/WN/WhoIs/story?id=3770445&page=1.
13. Quoted in Palmer, "Joe Biden," p. 39.
14. Quoted in Krawczeniuk, "Remembering His Roots."

15. Quoted in Crawford, "Joe Biden Fights Hard."
16. Quoted in Michael Rubinkam, "Biden's Scranton Childhood Left Lasting Impression," *USA Today*, August 27, 2008, www.usatoday.com/news/politics/2008-08-27-3524505538_x.htm.
17. Biden, *Promises to Keep*, p. 4.
18. Quoted in Broder, "Father's Tough Life an Inspiration for Biden."
19. Quoted in Crawford, "Joe Biden Fights Hard."
20. Quoted in Palmer, "Joe Biden," p. 165.

Chapter 2: College, Marriage, and Politics

21. Biden, *Promises to Keep*, p. 25.
22. Quoted in M.J. Stephey, "The Candidates in Print," *Time*, www.time.com/time/2007/candidates_books/biden.
23. Quoted in Lois Romano, "Joe Biden and the Politics of Belief; Ready to Announce for President, He Dismisses the Polls: 'I'm Going To Win,'" *Washington Post*, June 9, 1987.
24. Quoted in Brozyna, "Get to Know Joe Biden."
25. Biden, *Promises to Keep*, p. 27.
26. Quoted in Romano, "Joe Biden and the Politics of Belief."
27. Quoted in Palmer, "Joe Biden," p. 40.
28. Quoted in Stephey, "The Candidates in Print."
29. Quoted in Romano, "Joe Biden and the Politics of Belief."
30. Quoted in Lois Romano, "The Second Life of Joe Biden; After Campaign Disaster and a Near-Fatal Illness, a Calmer, More Resolute Senator," *Washington Post*, January 12, 1989.
31. Biden, *Promises to Keep*, p. 42.
32. Quoted in Romano, "Joe Biden and the Politics of Belief."
33. Quoted in Richardson, "Joe," p. 80.

Chapter 3: Triumph and Tragedy

34. Biden, *Promises to Keep*, p. 50.
35. Quoted in Brozyna, "Get to Know Joe Biden."
36. Quoted in Brian Naylor, "Biden's Road to Senate Took Tragic Turn," NPR, October 8, 2007, www.npr.org/templates/story/story.php?storyId=14999603.

37. Quoted in Rubinkam, "Biden's Scranton Childhood Left Lasting Impression."
38. Quoted in Naylor, "Biden's Road to Senate Took Tragic Turn."
39. Biden, *Promises to Keep*, p. 79.
40. Quoted in Biden, speech, Democratic National Convention.
41. Biden, *Promises to Keep*, p. 81.
42. Quoted in Brozyna, "Get to Know Joe Biden."
43. Quoted in Palmer, "Joe Biden," p. 40.
44. Quoted in Stephey, "The Candidates in Print."
45. Quoted in Brozyna, "Get to Know Joe Biden."
46. Quoted in Heidi Evans, "From a Blind Date to Second Lady, Jill Biden's Coming into Her Own," *New York Daily News*, December 28, 2008, www.nydailynews.com/news/politics/2008/12/27/2008-12-27_from_a_blind_date_to_second_lady_jill_bi.html?page=0.
47. Quoted in Romano, "Joe Biden and the Politics of Belief."
48. Quoted in Palmer, "Joe Biden," p. 42.

Chapter 4: Political Successes and Failures

49. Quoted in Romano, "Joe Biden and the Politics of Belief."
50. Biden, *Promises to Keep*, p. 110.
51. Quoted in *Time*, "Special Section: 200 Faces for the Future," *Time*, July 15, 1974, www.time.com/time/magazine/article/0,9171,879402-6,00.html.
52. Quoted in *Richmond Times*, "President Happy," *Richmond Times*, September 5, 1987.
53. Quoted in Robert Healy, "A Maverick Ponders '88 Race," *Boston Globe*, May 16, 1986.
54. Quoted in Romano, "Joe Biden and the Politics of Belief."
55. Quoted in Albert R. Hunt, "A Senator Strives to Make the Big Leagues," *Wall Street Journal*, April 7, 1986.
56. Quoted in Crawford, "Joe Biden Fights Hard."
57. Quoted in Robin Toner, "Biden 'Angry as Hell' over Latest Allegations," *Houston Chronicle*, September 21, 1987.
58. Quoted in Margaret Carlson, "Biden Is also Reborn," *Time*, September 12, 1988, www.time.com/time/magazine/article/0,9171,968383-1,00.html.

59. Quoted in Ruth Marcus, "Sen. Biden to Press Bork on His Criticism of Rulings; Burger Calls Such Questioning Improper," *Washington Post*, August 12, 1987.
60. Quoted in Lois Romano, "The Second Life of Joe Biden."
61. Quoted in Carlson, "Biden Is also Reborn."
62. Quoted in David S. Broder, "In '87, Biden Did 'the Wrong Things,' but Plans a Better '88," *Houston Chronicle*, January 2, 1988.

Chapter 5: The 2008 Presidential Campaign

63. Biden, *Promises to Keep*, p. xx.
64. Quoted in Stephey, "The Candidates in Print."
65. Joe Biden, interview by Tim Russert, *Meet the Press*, MSN, April 29, 2007, www.msnbc.msn.com/id/18381961.
66. Quoted in Stephey, "The Candidates in Print."
67. Quoted in Perry Bacon Jr., "Why Joe Biden Isn't Being Coy About Running for President," *Time*, August 2, 2006, www.time.com/time/nation/article/0,8599,1222255,00.html.
68. Quoted in Elisabeth Bumiller, "Biden Campaigning with Ease After Hardships," *New York Times*, December 14, 2007, www.nytimes.com/2007/12/14/us/politics/14biden.html?_r=1.
69. Quoted in Johanna Neuman and Stuart Silverstein, "All Eyes on VP Choice Biden; Obama Chose 'Dynamic' Partner, Clinton Says," *Los Angeles Times*, August 24, 2008, http://articles.latimes.com/2008/aug/24/nation/na-biden24.
70. Quoted in Neuman and Silverstein, "All Eyes on VP Choice Biden."
71. Quoted in Jason Horowitz, "Biden Unbound: Lays into Clinton, Obama, Edwards," *New York Observer*, February 4, 2007, www.observer.com/node/36658.
72. Quoted in Democratic presidential debate, moderated by George Stephanopoulos, *This Week*, ABC News, August 19, 2007, http://abcnews.go.com/Politics/Decision2008/story?id=3498294.
73. Quoted in Shailagh Murray, "Biden, Dodd Withdraw from Race," *Washington Post*, January 4, 2008.

74. Quoted in Neuman and Silverstein, "All Eyes on VP Choice Biden."
75. Quoted in Jill Lawrence and Martha T. Moore, "In Biden, a Life Story to Complement Obama's," *USA Today*, August 25, 2008, www.usatoday.com/news/politics/election2008/2008-08-24-obama-biden_N.htm.
76. Biden, speech, Democratic National Convention.
77. Quoted in Lawrence and Moore, "In Biden."
78. Quoted in Broder, "Father's Tough Life an Inspiration for Biden."
79. Biden, interview by Couric.
80. Quoted in David Lightman, "Joe Biden Won Veep Debate, Polls Say," *Tulsa World*, October 4, 2008.
81. Quoted in Randall Chase, "Delaware Crowds Welcome Biden Campaign, Season Ends with Winners, Losers in Traditional Parade," *South Florida Sun*, November 7, 2008.

Chapter 6: Becoming the Vice President of the United States

82. Quoted in Sabrina Eaton, "Obama Inauguration Train Picks up Joe Biden in Delaware," *Cleveland Plain Dealer*, January 17, 2009, http://blog.cleveland.com/openers/2009/01/obama_inauguration_train_picks.html.
83. Quoted in Jim Puzzanghera, Stacy St. Clair, and Christi Parons, "Obamas Get the Balls Rolling with Style; Barack Obama the 44th President of the United States of America; Obama's Inauguration," *(Baltimore, MD) Sun*, January 21, 2009.
84. Quoted in *Milwaukee Journal Sentinel*, "At Last, Obamas Have First Dance," *Milwaukee Journal Sentinel*, January 21, 2009.
85. Quoted in Ben Feller, "In Culminating Moment, Biden Is VP," *Connecticut Post*, January 20, 2009.
86. Quoted in Richardson, "Joe," p. 119.
87. Quoted in Alex Isenstadt, "GAO: Stimulus Funds Need More Oversight," *Politico*, April 23, 2009, www.politico.com/news/stories/0409/21642.html.
88. Joe Biden, speech, 45th Munich Security Conference, Munich, Germany, February 7, 2009, http://www.whitehouse.gov/

the_press_office/RemarksbyVicePresidentBidenat45thMuni chConferenceonSecurityPolicy/.

89. Joseph R. Biden, interview by Wolf Blitzer, *The Situation Room*, CNN, April 7, 2009, FDCH Political Transcripts, 04/07/2009. Accession No.: 32V3374075084.

90. Quoted in David Nather, "The Vice Presidency, According to Biden," *CQ Weekly*, April 5, 2009, www.cqpolitics.com/ wmspage.cfm?docid=weeklyreport-000003093487.

91. Quoted in Richardson, "Joe," p. 81.

92. Quoted in Palmer, "Joe Biden," p. 165.

93. Joe Biden, interview by Lesley Stahl, *60 Minutes*, CBS, April 26, 2009, www.cbsnews.com/stories/2009/04/24/ 60minutes/main4965941.shtml.

94. Quoted in Richardson, "Joe," p. 119.

1942

Joseph R. Biden Jr. is born on November 20, 1942, in Scranton, Pennsylvania.

1965

In June Biden graduates from the University of Delaware with a double major in history and political science.

1966

On August 27, 1966, Biden marries Neilia Hunter.

1968

Biden graduates from Syracuse University College of Law.

1970

On November 3 Biden is elected to New Castle County Council.

1972

On November 7 Biden is elected a U.S. senator from Delaware; on December 18 his wife and daughter are killed in an automobile accident.

1977

On June 17 Biden marries Jill Tracy Jacobs.

1987

On June 9 Biden announces his bid for the 1988 Democratic Party nomination for president; on September 23 Biden withdraws from the race.

1988

In February Biden is stricken with a brain aneurysm and it takes him eight months to recover from that and other health problems.

2007

On January 31 Biden announces his bid for the 2008 Democratic Party nomination for president; on August 1 Biden's memoir, *Promises to Keep: On Life and Politics*, is published.

2008

On January 3 Biden drops out of the presidential race; on August 23 Senator Barack Obama names Biden his vice presidential running mate; on November 4 Obama is elected president and Biden vice president; Biden is also reelected for the sixth time to his Senate seat.

2009

On January 3 Biden resigns his Senate seat so he can become vice president; on January 20 Biden is sworn in as the nation's forty-seventh vice president.

Books

Xander Cricket, *Joe Biden: A Neowonk Guide to the Vice President of the United States.* New York: CreateSpace, 2009. This book traces the career of Joe Biden and explains his position on many policy issues.

Nicole Iori, *People We Should Know: Joe Biden.* Milwaukee: Gareth Stevens, 2009. This is a biography of Joe Biden for younger readers.

Web Sites

New York Times (www.nytimes.com). A search of "Joe Biden" on this newspaper Web site offers "Times Topics: Joseph R. Biden Jr.," a page providing current *New York Times* stories about Biden as well as articles about the 2008 presidential election.

Organizing for America (http://www.barackobama.com/learn/meet_joe.php) Information about Vice President Joe Biden and the group that elected and still supports President Barack Obama politically.

The White House (www.whitehouse.gov). This Web site provides information about Joe Biden, including news releases, speeches, and photographs. The site also offers details about President Barack Obama and his administration, the White House and its history, and a comprehensive section about the U.S. government.

Boggs, J. Caleb, 37–38
Bork, Robert, 56, 56–58
Brain aneurysm, 11, 57, 58, 60–61
Brezhnev, Leonid, 51
Bush, George W., 64, 65, 66, 72

C
Campaigns
county council, 35
Owens, Valerie Biden, 39
presidential race (1987), 53, 53–56
presidential race (2008), 66–70, 71, 72–76, 74, 76
Senate race (1972), 37–38, 40–41
Carter, Jimmy, 51
Catholicism, 25–26, 30, 52
Cavel, Bert, 38
Ceremonial duties, 86, 87
Childhood
family life, 14–18
sports and friends, 21–23
stuttering, 9, 14
Children. See Biden, Ashley Blazer; Biden, Beau; Biden, Naomi Christina; Biden, Robert Hunter
Clinton, Hillary, 67–70, 78, 85
College, 25, 27–29, 30–31
Commuting, 10, 11, 45, 84
Comprehensive Crime Control Act, 52
Congress, work with, 85
County council, 37
Crime legislation, 52

D
Daredevil stunts, 22–23
Dating, 29–30, 47

Death of wife and daughter, 9, 11, 41–43, 45
Debates, 74–75, 76
Democratic Forum, 34–35
Democratic National Convention, 71, 72–73
Democratic party, 38
Des Moines speech, 54, 55–56
Draft, military, 33
Dukakis, Michael, 55

E
Eaton, John Henry, 42
Education
college, 25, 27–29, 30–31
high school, 19, 24
law school, 31–34
European leaders, meeting with, 83–85

F
Family
campaigning, 38
caring for sons, 45
childhood, 14–18
helping after wife's death, 47
lessons learned, 20
Senate campaign (1972), 40
vice presidency, 88–89
Fatherhood. See Parenting
Finnegan, Edward, 19
Finnegan household, 16–18
Football, 24
Ford, Gerald, 80
Foreign policy
Bush, George W., on policies of, 72
European leaders, meeting with, 83–85
experience, 11
Iraq War, 64–65

September 11th terrorist attacks, 62–64, *63*
Soviet Union, 51–52
Speech impediment, 9, 14, 17, 18–20, 24
Sports, 21–23, *22*, 24, *86*, 87
Stephanopoulos, George, 67
Study habits, 27–29, 31–33
Stuttering, 9, 14, 17, 18–20, 24
Sussex County Jamboree, 60
Syracuse University College of Law, 31–34

T
Talking, 9, 11–12
Terrorist attacks, 62–64
Topen, Henry, 38
Train travel, *10*, 11, 45, 77, 88

U
Union workers, 73
University of Delaware, 25, 27–29, *28*

V
Vice presidency, 79–85
Vice presidential candidacy, 68, 70, 72–76
Vietnam War, 32, 33–34, 41

W
Walsh, David, 34
Walsh, E. John, 24
Walter Reed Army Medical Center, 61
Weaver, Gregg, 77
White House Task Force on Middle Class Families, 83, *85*, 88
Working class voters, 73

About the Author

Michael V. Uschan has written over seventy books, including *Life of an American Soldier in Iraq*, for which he won the 2005 Council for Wisconsin Writers Juvenile Nonfiction Award. Uschan began his career as a writer and editor with United Press International, a wire service that provided stories to newspapers, radio, and television. He considers writing history books a natural extension of the skills he developed in his many years as a journalist. Uschan and his wife, Barbara, reside in the Milwaukee suburb of Franklin, Wisconsin.